FREEPORT PUBLIC LIBRARY
100 E. Douglas
Freeport, IL 610

DEC 1 2 2016     W9-AVR-748

# VICTORIAN FANCY STITCHERY
## Techniques & Designs

Edited by
### Flora Klickmann

Dover Publications, Inc.
Mineola, New York

*Bibliographical Note*

This Dover edition, first published in 2003, is a slightly abridged reprint of The Home Art Book of Fancy Stitchery, published by "The Girl's Own Paper & Woman's Magazine," London, n.d. Some advertisements appearing in the original edition have been omitted.

*Library of Congress Cataloging-in-Publication Data*

Victorian fancy stitchery : techniques & designs / edited by Flora Klickmann.
    p. cm.
  Reprint. Originally published under title: The home art book of fancy stitchery. London : Girl's Own Paper & Woman's Magazine.
  ISBN 0-486-43271-8 (pbk.)
    1. Fancy work. 2. Needlework, Victorian. I. Klickmann, Flora.

TT750.V53 2003
746.4—dc22

                                 2003055669

Manufactured in the United States of America
Dover Publications, Inc., 31 East 2nd Street, Mineola, N.Y. 11501

# The Home Art Book
## of Fancy Stitchery

ESTABLISHED 1846.

# Wools

### for KNITTING and NEEDLEWORK of every Description.

## ART NEEDLEWORK,

### The Latest Styles as produced.

## RELIABLE MATERIALS of all kinds.

CANVASSES, FABRICS, TRIMMINGS, SILKS, COTTONS, THREADS, ARTIFICIAL SILKS, AND LUSTRE YARNS FOR ALL PURPOSES.

## JEVONS & MELLOR,

### Corporation St. & Old Square, BIRMINGHAM.

Price Lists, Patterns Post Free.

# THE
# Home Art Book
OF
# Fancy Stitchery

With samples of Drawn Thread Work, Resille Net, Bead-work and Fancy Stitches for Dress Trimmings, Feather Stitching, Hardanger Work, Hedebo Work, Knitting, Macramé Work, Darned Net, Cross-stitch, Ancient Cut-Work, Embroidery on Flannel.

EDITED BY

## FLORA KLICKMANN

*Editor of " The Girl's Own Paper & Woman's Magazine."*

London:

The Office of "The Girl's Own Paper & Woman's Magazine
4 Bouverie Street, & 65 St. Paul's Churchyard E.C.

# A
# Happy Combination.

Beauty and reliability go hand in hand where Beehive Wools are used in the production of articles for wear or for ornament. Beehive Wools present an almost unlimited choice of styles, colours, and textures for all kinds of plain and fancy knitting. In appearance, quality and durability

# BEEHIVE Wools

## ARE ABSOLUTELY UNSURPASSED

for supreme quality in all kinds of Knitting, Fingering and Rug Wools. Send 1½d. in stamps for "Guide to Knitting and Crochet."

# J. & J. BALDWIN

& Partners Ltd., HALIFAX, Est⁰ 1785

Eng.

REGISTERED

TRADE MARK

# A Handsome Tea=cloth.

THE CLOTH COMPLETE.

We illustrate here a Five o'clock Cloth of unusually handsome design. It is made of the most transparent lawn and very fine crochet, and is an illustration of what needlework wonders can be accomplished if patience, care and evenness of stitch be brought to bear on the work. The actual crochet-patterns are composed of really simple stitches. We are not giving exhaustive instructions in this case, but merely supplying a few details that will be sufficient to enable any girl who has had practice in crochet to copy the cloth from the pictures.

As will be seen, five square insets are let into the lawn, and four rings or medallions are applied to the lawn ; in the latter case the lawn is not cut away at the back. The edge is composed of these same rings laid on lawn backgrounds, and the same pattern edges the slightly scalloped edge of the cloth itself.

## The Narrow Insertion Outlining the Squares.

*1st Row.*—Ch 18, 1 tr into the 9th ch from needle, * ch 3, 1 tr into 3rd ch from last tr. Repeat twice from *. You should now have a row of 4 sp.

*2nd Row.*—Turn with 6 ch, 1 tr into top of tr in previous row, 2 tr into sp, 1 tr into top of next tr, 3 tr into sp, 1 tr into next tr, 3 ch, 1 tr into 3rd chain so as to end the row with a square sp.

*3rd Row.*—6 ch, 1 tr into each of the 8 tr in previous row, 3 ch, 1 tr.

1

# A Handsome Tea-cloth.

THE SQUARE INSET.

## The Loop Design in Centre of Square.

If the small detail of this part of the design is studied carefully, it will be seen that d c's are worked round the edge of the narrow insertion, 3 d c into each sp, while at every 4th sp occur 3 loops of 18 ch each. These loops are in turn held together by strands of 12 ch each, with 12 d c worked over each at the next round. These sets will lessen as the work proceeds, simply by omitting the connecting strand of 12 ch at each corner. The looser strands, which are caught together between the groups of loops, consist of 18 ch each.

*4th Row.*—6 ch, 1 tr (this forms one sp), then make 3 more sp as in 1st row.

*5th Row.*—1 sp, 8 tr, 1 sp (like 2nd row).

*6th Row.*—6 ch, 4 tr, then 2 sp.

*7th Row.*—Like 5th row.

*8th Row.*—2 sp, 4 tr, 1 sp.

Repeat from 5th row.

Notice that each side of the square must start with the four open sp, then the solid block formed by the 8 tr in rows 2 and 3, so as to make a good corner. The four sides are worked without breaking the thread, the final edges being sewn together.

A CORNER OF THE CLOTH.

## The Round Medallions in Border and let into the Cloth.

Ch 7, then back into the very first ch, work 2 tr, 3 ch, 2 tr, 3 ch, 2 tr, 3 ch, 2 tr.

* Turn with 6 ch, and into the first little sp in previous row work 2 tr, 3 ch, 2 tr, 3 ch, 2 tr, 3 ch, 2 tr. Repeat from * till you have 14 scallops on one side and 13 scallops on the other. Then join in a ring, having the 14 scallops on the outside and the 13 on the inside of the ring.

Now work 5 d c into the first large sp on the outside edge (made by the 6 ch you turned with), then 5 d c into the next sp, 5 d c into the 3rd sp, and 1 d c down into the root of trs.

Next ch 7, and carry it down to the large sp on the inner side of

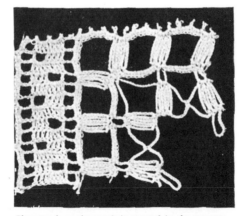

Showing how the work is started in the squares.

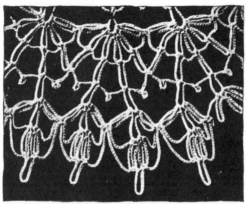

A Detail of the Outside Border.

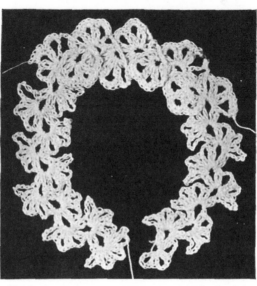

The Design used in the Medallions and in the Borders.

## A Handsome Teacloth.

the circle (this sp will be just a trifle in advance of the one above that you have just filled in with d c's). Fill in this first sp with 5 d c, and (going backwards along the work) make 5 d c into the next 2 sp, and 1 d c again into the root of the trs.

You have now put d c into what may be called both sides of one scallop.

Now ch 7, and cross with this right over to the outer edge of the circle, and proceed to fill in with d c the top of the next scallop.

In this way work all round the ring. If you study the illustration showing this ring in detail, you will see that part of it is without this extra cross-bar working, while the centre portion has the d c started, and

3

## A Handsome Tea-cloth.

the 7 ch crossing over the work can be seen.

It is more convenient if the extra d c and cross ch are worked before the strip is actually joined in a ring.

This ring forms the round medallion on the cloth; it is also used in the border. This design also edges the lawn and serves to unite it to the border.

### The Edge of the Cloth.

To make the open-work ring round medallions already described in the border, * make two loops of 18 ch each into the centre-point of one of the scallops. Ch 9, catch back into the fifth loop, making a picot loop. Then ch 5 which carries you to the next scallop. Repeat from *.

*2nd Row.*—Make a d c into the bottom of each of the 2 loops already made. Ch 4, catch into picot loop above, ch 18, catch back into picot loop, ch 4, then make a d c into each loop above and repeat all round. Catch into the table-cloth edge and to the next medallion where shown in the illustration.

You will see by looking at the corner illustrated that each medallion is surrounded with this open-work circle.

For the outside edge of the border, work as follows :

*1st Row.*—Into the long loop of 18 ch already made, make 6 loops of 18 ch, then ch 18 to carry you to the next loop of 18, where you make 6 more loops. In this way proceed round the cloth.

*2nd Row.*—The outside loop of every group of six is caught to the 18 ch, which connects the sets to-

gether. (See small detail of outside border). Ch 7 from this point and catch into the next loop, Into this make another loop of 18 ch, 5 ch between the next loop, and another loop of 18 ch. Complete the row in this way with 4 loops of 18 ch to each little scallop.

*3rd Row.*—The first and the last loop of each scallop are caught together with a d c into each loop, then ch 9, catch back into fourth ch. Ch 5, catch into loop above. Into this same loop make another loop of 18 ch. One more connecting picot ch, another loop of 18 ch, 2 picot ch, then start the next scallop in the same way.

*4th Row.*—Into each of the 2 loops above make 3 loops of 18 ch each, connect with a between ch of 18.

*5th Row.*—Into the middle of the 3 loops again make 3 loops of 18 ch. Then ch 12 to connect the third loop to the between ch, and another 12 to carry you to the loop in the centre of the next 3.

*6th Row.*—A d c into each of the 3 loops, from the middle loop make another loop of 18 ch, then ch 18 and carry to the centre of the between ch. Another 18 ch brings you down to the next group of loops.

Several of the features of this cloth could be employed in other ways. The square insets would make very pretty pin-cushion tops. The insertion round the squares could be used in household linen. The pattern used for the medallions would in itself make a very pretty edge, and looks well worked in two shades of cotton. The outside border to the cloth would be a handsome decoration without any other addition.

*For a Fine Cloth, use Barbour's No. 120 Lace Thread.*

*Beautiful Lawn can be obtained from*
*Messrs. Robinson & Cleaver, 42 R, Donegal Place, Belfast.*

# Soutache Braiding on Net.

Soutache braid embroidered on net is much used for trimming costumes, blouses, coats, etc.

The work is easily done and very effective. Net of any kind and in every shade can be used, with the braid to correspond in fineness, and in colour to match or contrast with the material trimmed.

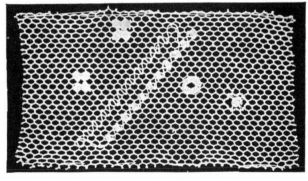

Stitches that could be used with the braiding.

The design is first copied on the usual glazed calico, or stout paper answers very well, then the net is carefully tacked over the pattern, next place the braid over the outline and neatly sew to the net, putting the stitches through the centre of the braid and using a fine thread.

The embroidery is further embellished with a few motifs in crochet worked with thread to match the braid.

In the piece here illustrated a small padded ring is worked over in d c

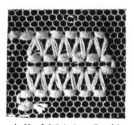

A Useful Stitch to Combine with Braid.

with ivory white silk which matches the colour of the silk braid employed.

When all the outline has been gone over, cut the threads on the back of the paper pattern, and remove the lace, then press with a hot iron on the back to complete it.

If you are doing a long strip for insertion, you will need to cut the threads when one section is finished and go on tacking the net down on to the same piece of pattern till the strip is complete.

The top illustration shows several motifs that could be worked on net and combined with the braiding.

Be very careful in working not to draw the thread too tight.

Good Net can be obtained from Messrs. S. Peach & Co., The Looms, Nottingham.

Soutache Braid and Crochet Rings.

# Embroidery on Net.

Embroidery on net is very popular now for trimming blouses, camisole tops and the finer kinds of lingerie. All grades of net are employed, from the finest Brussels to heavy filet, and the threads used to embroider them match

This would make a good border for curtains.

the net in texture. Silk, vegetable silk, or mercerised cotton, white or tinted, are all employed for this class of work. The introduction of the crochet edge has a strengthening effect on the work.

Some suggestions for "filling-in" stitches. Long lines of darning like this are striking and not tedious to work.

Patterns like the above are very effective.

These designs are simple and wear well.

A row of chain can be worked through the second last row of meshes and then a row of double crochet and picots, or any other device, worked over the edge through the centre of the chain stitches.

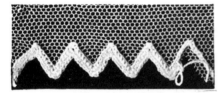

Edgings, insertions, or motifs can be finished at the edge with buttonhole stitches or a crochet finish.

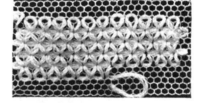

A very useful stitch for " filling-in " is illustrated above.

It is usual to use a coarser thread for the outline than for the filling, or the filling thread may be doubled for the purpose.

For summer Casement or Bris bris curtains, this work is exceedingly light and pretty. Here the coarser net is quite as effective as the finer makes, and is much easier to work upon, the large mesh simplifying the counting of the holes.

Be careful not to draw the working thread too tightly, or the net will pucker; even work is to be aimed at.

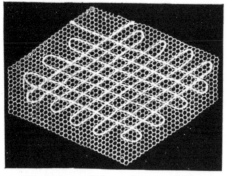

This design could be used as a medallion, or repeated to form a border.

A design that is quickly worked. It makes good bands of trimming.

Crochet edges do much to strengthen the work; but here again care must be taken not to draw the thread too tightly. Single crochet into each mesh is as good a foundation for crochet edge as any; then if desired a deeper edge can be worked on to this. Be careful, however, not to make the crochet edge too deep or too heavy, otherwise it will weight down the net.

Another good finish to curtains is a broad hem, simply run down with the linen thread or mercerised cotton.

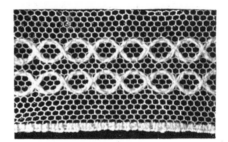

Both these edges are finished with crochet.

# Designs for Lacy Woollen Scarfs.

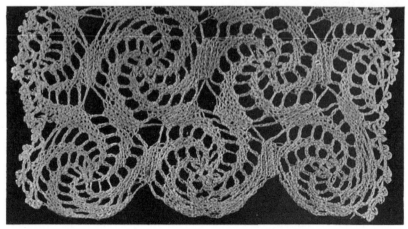

COGWHEEL DESIGN.

For these scarfs we recommend Baldwin's Beehive Pyrenees Wool, which is as fine a wool as you can obtain, and delightfully soft and charming in appearance.

### Cog-wheel Design.

Use a No. 1 steel crochet - hook, making 8 ch, which form into a ring, 5 ch, 2 d c into the ring six times, forming six loops.

*2nd Round.*—5 ch, 3 d c into each loop.

*3rd Round.*—5 ch, omit the first 2 d c in preceding loop, 1 d c into the third d c, 3 d c over the ch stitches.

*4th Round.*—In this and each succeeding round put 5 ch between the groups of d c, omit first two in each group, 1 d c into each of the other d c, and 3 d c over the ch. There are eight rounds in each motif, and they are connected by a row of single stitch on the wrong side in two adjoining groups of d c.

In every second row it will be necessary to work exactly half a motif, to fill the spaces at each side. For

this, start on the ring centre, putting only three loops into it, then work on these, breaking off the thread at the end of each row after fastening it off neatly, and starting at the beginning again, preserving the pattern of the motif.

Finish the edges with a row of 10 ch loops, fastened with 2 d c, and in the half motif these 2 d c should be worked over the ends of the rows. Into the loops put two 6 ch picots, each fastened with a d c, and put 3 ch between the loops. Continue the 10 ch loops around the ends, and finish with a deep fringe knotted twice.

For the fringe, wind the thread around a piece of stout cardboard six inches deep (or a book of the required size will do), cut the threads along one edge, take eight strands, and putting the ends evenly together, insert the loop through one of the loops in the end of the scarf, run the ends of thread through the loop and draw up the knot. When all the loops are filled in this way, take the four strands of the first group at the right hand side, and the next four of the second group, twist around to form a loop, and insert the ends through this loop, then pull up the knot gradually, until it is about three-quarters of an inch from the first knot ; it is pulled tightly here to secure it. Form a second row in the same way, then cut the ends evenly to finish it.

### Scroll Design.

In this design two colours are used. It is in the well-known hairpin work for the lighter colour, and ch stitches for the connection and the darker. Use a three - quarter - inch hairpin staple, make a ch stitch with the crochet - hook, catch this with the thumb and middle finger of the left hand in the centre of the staple, having the prongs turned from you.

Keep the thread over the fingers as in plain crochet, with the staple between it and the hook, bring the hook with the stitch on it to the centre of the staple, having the thread around the right prong, draw the thread through the stitch, turn the staple round on the hand to the left, thus bringing the thread around the other prong, hook the thread through the stitch on the needle, and make 2 d c on the upper thread of the loop on the left prong, * turn the prong again to the left, hook the thread through the stitch on the needle, 2 d c on next loop, and repeat from *.

Make a long strip, then with the darker thread make a d c in the last loop at one side, * 6 ch, 1 d c into next loop, repeat the 6 ch into each of next nine loops, 1 d c into each of

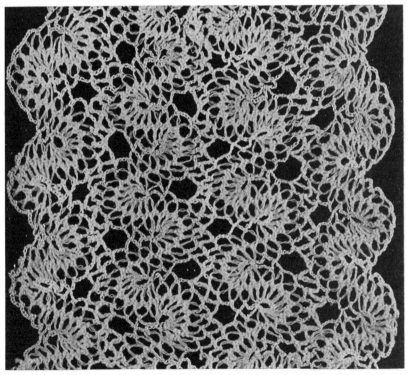

A LATTICE-WORK DESIGN.

next nine loops, 1 d c through the first of these to form a ring, and repeat from *, connecting the second loop to the corresponding loop at the opposite side in the centre.

Repeat this row at the other side, putting the 10 d c into the loops between the rings of first row. When four strips are worked, place two together, and connect with a row of 3 ch from loop to loop at opposite sides. The two top loops over a mitre are connected with a d c, in order to span the space at the other side.

The ends of this scarf may be drawn up to a point, and a cord made of twisted threads of both colours inserted, from which a large tassel may be suspended.

## Lattice-work Design.

In this design, also hairpin work, only one colour is used, and the strip is very long, only one being required. Do not break off the thread at the end of the hairpin work until near the end of the last row in the scarf. Insert the hook at the back of each loop to give it a twisted appearance, 1 d c, * 5 ch, 1 d c into each loop at one side, repeat from * for the length of the scarf. 9 d c into next nine loops, 2 ch, 1 d c into last ch loop, 2 ch, 1 d c into next loop in the hairpin work, * 2 ch, 1 d c into next ch loop at opposite side, 2 ch, 1 d c into next hairpin loop, and repeat from * to the end, then turn as before with the 10 consecutive d c. There are eight rows connected in this way. The sides are finished with 1 d c, 9 ch, 1 d c into each loop, 1 ch between the loops.

Finish the ends in the same way, and add a deep fringe as directed in the first design.

TO avoid "ladders"—where the wool runs slack at the needle ends—when knitting a stocking, slip the last stitch from each knitting needle on to the next needle, and knit it as the commencement of the new row. If this is always done, the stocking will show uniform knitting throughout, with no trace of "ladders."

# Ideas for Handkerchiefs.

The girl who introduces a distinctive note into her personal belongings, nowadays, is noted by her friends. We get so used to seeing machine-made goods that are turned out by tens of thousands that it is positively refreshing to see something that is a little off the beaten track.

Now here are some new ideas for girls who like pretty handkerchiefs and yet do not care for those betrimmed with cheap

lace and badly-done embroidery that are all too plentiful in the present day. And it is interesting to notice that these trimmings were made from oddments that appeared to be of no further use, though, of course, there can be no objection to new trimmings being made on purpose. The main thing is to see that they are of very fine make.

The ornaments on the handkerchief at the top right hand and the one above are fragments of an old-fashioned collar made of fine tatting. The little

motifs were cut out and appliquéd to the linen, which was afterwards cut away from the back. The little "baby" edging was taken from the extreme edge of the collar. The corner just below shows how some odd motifs from another lace collarette were used—one in each corner—to smarten a handkerchief.

This suggests possibilities for tiny designs in very fine crochet or tatting. Or fragments from pieces of real lace that are too small for any other purpose would look very pretty and lacy used on lawn.

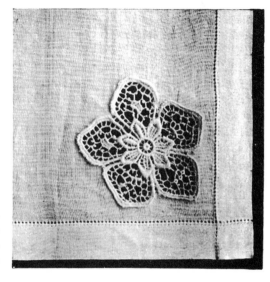

# Pretty Featherstitchings.

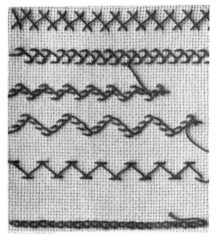

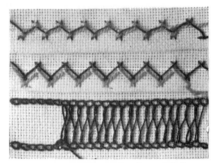

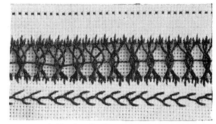

7 and 8. Double Herring-bone Stitch.
9. A Pretty Filling Stitch.

24. A Design in Faggoting Stitch.

1. Herring-bone Stitch.
2. Single Coral Stitch.
3. Double Coral Stitch.
4. Treble Coral Stitch.
5. An Uncommon Fancy Stitch.
6. Plain Chain Stitch.

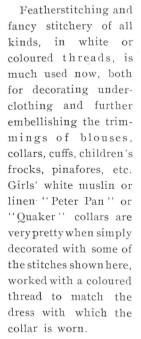

Featherstitching and fancy stitchery of all kinds, in white or coloured threads, is much used now, both for decorating underclothing and further embellishing the trimmings of blouses, collars, cuffs, children's frocks, pinafores, etc. Girls' white muslin or linen " Peter Pan " or "Quaker" collars are very pretty when simply decorated with some of the stitches shown here, worked with a coloured thread to match the dress with which the collar is worn.

For decorating the napery of a "girl's own" bedroom nothing

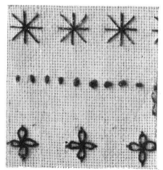

10. Star Stitch.
11. French Knots.
12. Tied Loop Stitch.

13. Coil or Bullion Stitch.
14. Open Loop Stitch.

*Arden's " Star Sylko" is excellent for this work. It comes in two sizes, Medium and Fine, and in a wide range of colours.*

can give such satisfactory results from the little work required as this fancy stitching. Pillows, cushions, toilet covers and mats, and even bedspreads can all be quickly made to match the general scheme of colour of the rest of the furnishings, and mercerised threads can be had in almost every known shade of colour.

*No. 1.* Herring-bone stitch. This stitch is worked from left to right. Insert the needle horizontally from right to left and make a stitch, bring the thread down to the right and make another stitch in the same way, having the needle to come out under where the last went in the line above; the threads cross each other diagonally.

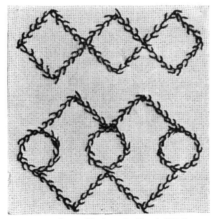

20 *and* 21. Designs in Coral Stitch.

No. 2 is the single coral stitch, which is worked vertically; the stitches may be any size but must be uniform. Bring the thread up in the centre, form it into a loop, which hold down with the left thumb, insert the needle on the left a short distance from where it came up, and bring it out in a slanting direction over the held-down thread; repeat this stitch to the right and continue from left to right alternately.

Nos. 3 & 4 are double and treble coral stitch worked in the same way as the first but with two and three stitches at each side respectively. This stitch is the most general in use and can be worked up into

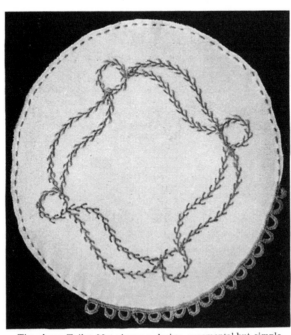

The above Toilet Mat shows a design, ornamental but simple, for decorating a set of napery for a girl's bedroom, and is just a suggestion for a variety of other designs, which can easily be carried out from the foregoing.

circles, diamonds, and various other designs for insertions, belts and other trimmings.

No. 5. This fancy stitch is used either alone or in a repetition of rows close together for filling in spaces. It is worked from left to right, horizontally, and can easily be copied from the illustration.

No. 6 is plain chain stitch.

Nos. 7 and 8 are double herring-boning, worked on a wide stitch in different colours; in the first the second thread is worked around the crossing portions of the first row, and in the last the two rows are worked close together.

No. 9. A pretty filling stitch; this is just two rows of ch with a row of herring-bone worked from side to side on the inner loop of the chs.

No. 10. Star stitch, taken from the centre and carried back underneath to the centre again

*No.* 11. French knot stitch, in which you bring out the thread where the knot is to be, then insert the point of the needle at the same place from underneath and wind the thread around it three or four times, pull the needle through all the loops and tighten the knot; insert the needle down behind the knot and bring it up again where the next knot is to be.

*No.* 12. Tied loop stitch is just a loop held in the centre with a stitch over the thread.

*No.* 13. Coil or bullion stitch, in which the thread is wound several times around the needle.

*No.* 14. Open loop stitch, held down in the centre with a stitch over.

*No.* 15. Wheat-ear stitch is worked on a central stem of single coral stitch; it is a loop placed in the central stitch and held in place at the top with a stitch over.

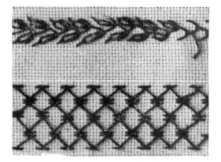
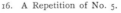

15   Wheat Ear Stitch.
16. A Repetition of No. 5.

22 *and* 23.  Designs in Coral Stitch.

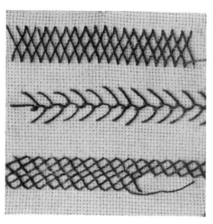

17. A Variation of the Herring-bone.
18. Fishbone Stitch.
19. Another Variety of the Herring-bone.

*No.* 16. This is the same as No. 5, worked closely together to form a filling.

*No.* 17. This is worked like herring-bone but close up together.

*No.* 18. Fish-bone stitch, worked like single coral stitch but with the outside stitches much longer.

*No.* 19. Another variety of the herring-bone, but worked close together in rows to form a filling.

*Nos.* 20, 21, 22, and 23 are designs for insertion, edging or filling, in the ever-useful single coral stitch.

*No.* 24 is a design in "faggoting" stitch, useful for joining two pieces of different kinds, or for connecting a strip of insertion with material: it is composed of 3 buttonhole stitches, one short at each side of a longer one, then the thread carried to the opposite side and three stitches formed there, and so on alternately.

# A Border for a Tea=cloth.

This lace is worked in Manlove's Irish Lace Thread No. 42, with wheels of fine braid, or coarser braid and Ardern's Crochet Cotton No. 36.

*Note.*—"1 tr"=long treble throughout.

Sew at bar of braid 8 ovals. Work middle part first as follows :—

*1st Row.*—* 2 tr into first loop of braid, 7 ch, 1 d c into next, 3 ch, 1 d c into next, 3 ch, 1 d c, 3 ch, 1 d c, 7 ch, 2 tr. Repeat from * all round.

*2nd Row.*—2 tr into 7 ch, 7 ch, 1 d c into loop of 3 ch, 3 ch, 1 d c into next sp of 3 ch, 3 ch, 1 d c into next, 7 ch, 2 tr into 7 ch. Repeat from beginning.

*3rd Row.*—2 tr into 7 ch, 7 ch, 1 d c into sp of 3 ch, 3 ch, 1 d c into next, 7 ch, 2 tr into 7 ch. Repeat from beginning.

*4th Row.*—2 d c into 7 ch, 8 ch, catch in fourth ch from needle to form picot, 4 ch, 2 d c into 7 ch. Repeat.

**Outside Edge.**

*1st Row.*—* 5 l tr (*i.e.*, 5 long treble) into first loop of braid, 7 ch, 1 d c into next, 3 ch, 1 d c into next, 3 ch, 1 d c into next, 3 ch, 1 d c into next, 7 ch, 5 l tr into last loop, 9 ch, 5 d c over bar, 9 ch. Repeat from *. Finish round with 9 ch, join to first 1 tr, single crochet along the tr.

*2nd Row.*—5 l tr into 7 ch, 9 ch, 1 d c into first 3 ch, 3 ch, 1 d c, 3 ch, 1 d c, 9 ch, 5 l tr into 7 ch, 7 ch, 1 d c into 9 ch, 1 d c into next 9 ch. Repeat from beginning and finish round as before.

*3rd Row.*—9 d c down 9 ch, 1 d c into sp of 3 ch, 3 ch, 1 d c into next 9 d c up 9 ch, 9 ch, 5 l tr into 7 ch, 10 ch, 1 d c between the 2 d c over bar, 10 ch, 5 l tr, 9 ch. Repeat from beginning,

*4th Row.*—5 l tr into 9 ch, 3 ch, 5 l tr into next 9 ch, 9 ch, 9 d c down 9 ch, 1 d c into first d c of last row, 8 ch, 1 d c on top of last d c of previous row, 9 d c into 9 ch. Repeat from beginning.

*5th Row.*—Into the 3 ch between groups of 5 l tr work 5 l tr, 9 ch, 9 d c into 9 ch, 1 d c into first d c of

## A Border for a Tea-cloth.

previous 8 ch, catch back into fourth ch to form picot, 4 ch, 1 d c into ninth d c, 8 d c into 8 ch, 1 d c into d c, 4 ch, picot of 4 ch as before, 4 ch, 1 d c into last d c, 9 d c into 9 ch, 9 ch. Repeat from beginning of row.

When working the other wheels, join when making the 9 ch after 5 1 tr. Continue working unfinished wheel until the 9 ch before 5 1 tr is reached, where again join.

### Lower Border.

When the required length is obtained, work border as follows :—

*1st Row.*—2 d c into 2 centre d c of 8 d c between points, 9 ch, 1 d c into picot, 9 ch, 1 d c into centre of 9 d c, 9 ch (top of point is now reached), 1 1 tr, 5 ch, 2 1 tr into 9 ch, 2 ch, 2 1 tr into first 1 tr, 2 ch, 2 1 tr into third 1 tr, 2 ch, 2 1 tr into fifth 1 tr, 2 ch, 2 1 tr, 5 ch, 1 1 tr into 9 ch, 9 ch, 1 d c into middle of 9 d c, 9 ch, 1 d c into picot, 9 ch. Repeat once. 2 d c into 2 centre d c of 8 d c, 1 d c into picot, 9 ch, 1 d c into centre of 9 d c, 9 ch, 1 d c into ch, 9 ch, 1 d c into ch of next wheel and work round wheel to match the one just worked. Always break off and start same end of work.

*2nd Row.*—3 1 tr into first 9 ch of previous row, 9 ch, 3 d c into next 9 ch, 9 ch, 5 1 tr into 9 ch, 3 1 tr into 5 ch, * 2 ch, 2 1 tr into 2 ch. Repeat from * 3 times. 2 ch, 3 1 tr into 5 ch, 9 ch, 7 1 tr into 9 ch, 9 ch, 3 d c into 9 ch, 9 ch, 3 1 tr into 9 ch. Repeat from beginning of row once. 3 1 tr into 9 ch, 9 ch, 3 d c into 9 ch, 9 ch, 3 1 tr into 9 ch, 3 1 tr into 9 ch between wheels. Repeat from beginning of row to end of work.

*3rd Row.*—3 d c into first 9 ch, 9 ch, 3 d c into 9 ch, 9 ch, 8 1 tr into 9 ch, 9 ch, * 2 1 tr, 2 ch. Repeat from * 3 times. 2 1 tr into next 2 ch, 9 ch, 8

1 tr into 9 ch, 9 ch, 3 d c into 9 ch, 9 ch, 3 d c into 9 ch, 6 d c into 6 1 tr, 3 d c into next 9 ch, 9 ch. Repeat from beginning once, 3 d c into 9 ch, 3 ch, 3 d c into same 9 ch, 3 d c into next 9 ch, 9 d c into 9 1 tr, 3 d c into 9 ch, 3 d c, 3 ch, 3 d c into next 9 ch. Work next wheels to match the one just worked.

*4th Row.*—3 d c into first 9 ch, 9 d c into next 9 ch, 9 ch, 8 1 tr, 9 ch, 2 1 tr into 2 ch, 2 ch, 2 1 tr, 2 ch, 2 1 tr, 2 ch, 2 1 tr, 9 ch, 8 1 tr into 9 ch, 9 ch, 9 d c into next 9 ch, 3 d c on 3 d c, 7 d c into next 9 ch, 1 d c on each of the d c's of previous row, 7 d c. Repeat from beginning once, but between the third and fourth d c of the bar 7 work picot of 4 ch, 3 d c into 9 ch, 9 d c on 9 d c of previous row. Work next wheel to match the one just worked.

*5th Row.*—* 9 d c into ch before 8 1 tr of previous row, 9 ch, 8 1 tr, 9 ch, 2 1 tr into 2 ch, 2 ch, 2 1 tr into next 2 ch, 2 ch, 2 1 tr, 9 ch, 8 1 tr, 9 ch, 9 d c into next 9 ch, 9 d c into next, 3 d c on 3 d c, 9 ch, 1 d c into first d c, 4 ch, picot of 4 ch, 4 ch, 1 d c into last d c, 9 ch, ** 1 d c on the last d c of next group of 7, 1 d c on first of the next, 4 ch, picot 4 ch. Repeat from * to ** once, 4 ch, picot, 4 ch, 1 s c into picot of last row, 4 ch, picot, 4 ch, 1 d c into middle d c of previous row. Work next wheel to match.

*6th Row.*—* 9 d c into 9 ch before 8 1 tr, 9 ch, 8 1 tr, 9 ch, 2 1 tr into 2 ch, 2 ch, 2 1 tr into next 2 ch, 9 ch, 8 1 tr, 9 ch, 9 d c, 4 ch, picot 4 ch, 1 d c into ch before picot of last row, 4 ch, picot, 4 ch, 5 1 tr into 9 ch, ** miss 4 ch, picot 4 ch, and work 5 1 tr into next 9 ch, 4 ch, picot 4 ch, 1 d c into ch after picot, 4 ch, picot,

4 ch. Repeat from * to ** once, 4 ch, picot 4 ch, 1 d c into ch after picot, 4 ch, picot 4 ch, 1 d c into ch before picot. Work remainder of wheels to match.

*7th Row.*—* 1 d c into first d c of previous row, 4 ch, picot 4 ch, 9 d c into 9 ch, 4 ch, picot 4 ch, 8 1 tr into 9 ch, 1 picot, 8 1 tr into next 9 ch, 4 ch, picot 4 ch, 9 d c, 4 ch, picot 4 ch, 1 d c into ch before picot, 4 ch, picot 4 ch, 1 d c into ch, 4 ch, picot 4 ch, 4 1 tr between 1 tr of previous row, ** 4 1 tr between next 5 1 tr, 4 ch, picot 4 ch, 1 d c into ch after picot 4 ch, picot 4 ch, 1 d c into ch. Repeat from * to ** once, 4 ch, picot 4 ch, 1 d c into ch before picot, 4 ch, picot 4 ch, 1 d c after picot. Work next wheels to match.

**Upper Border.**

Two whole points and a part of those on either side are used for this border.

*1st Row.*—2 1 tr into last picot of point before the two middle points, 12 ch, 2 1 tr into picot of next point. 14 ch, 2 1 tr into 9 ch before 5 1 tr, 2 ch, 2 tr into second 1 tr, 2 ch, 2 tr into fourth tr, 2 ch, 2 tr into 9 ch, 14 ch, 2 1 tr into picot, 12 ch, 2 1 tr into next picot, 14 ch, 2 tr into 9 ch, 2 ch, 2 tr into second 1 tr, 2 ch, 2 tr into fourth 1 tr, 2 ch, 2 tr into 9 ch, 14 ch, 2 1 tr into picot, 12 ch, 2 1 tr into next picot, 12 ch, 2 1 tr into ch, 10 ch, 2 1 tr into ch. Repeat row to end of wheels. Break off.

*2nd Row.*—Always start same end of work, * 2 1 tr into ch, 9 ch, 4 1 tr into 14 ch, 9 ch, 2 tr into 2 ch, 2 ch, 2 tr, 2 ch, 2 tr, 9 ch, 3 d c into ch, 9 ch, 3 d c into next ch, 9 ch, 3 d c, 9 ch, 2 tr into 2 ch, 2 ch, 2 tr, 2 ch, 2 tr, 9 ch, 4 1 tr, 9 ch, 2 1 tr, 9 ch, 2 1 tr into 2 ch, 2 1 tr into ch, 2 1 tr into ch, 9 ch. Repeat from * to end of wheels. Break off.

*3rd Row.*—1 tr into ch, * 9 ch, 3 1 tr (1 between each of the 4 1 tr of last row), 9 ch, 2 tr into ch, 9 ch, 2 tr, 2 ch, 2 tr, 9 ch, 2 tr, 9 ch, 2 tr, 9 ch, 2 tr, 9 ch, 2 tr, 9 ch, 2 tr into 2 ch, 2 ch, 2 tr, 2 ch, 9 ch, 3 1 tr as before, 9 ch, 2 1 tr between the 2 1 tr of last row, 9 ch, 1 1 tr between 2 1 tr. 1 1 tr between next 2 1 tr, 1 1 tr between next 2 1 tr, 9 ch, 2 1 tr upon 2 1 tr. Repeat from *.

*4th Row.*—* 2 tr into ch, 9 ch. Repeat from * 11 times. 2 tr, 5 ch, 2 tr, 5 ch. Repeat from beginning of row.

*5th Row.*—Fill each space with d c.

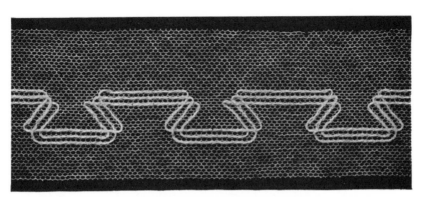

A GOOD BORDER DESIGN FOR DARNED NET CASEMENT CURTAINS.

# Trifles made from Handkerchiefs.

A JABOT MADE OF ONE HANDKERCHIEF.

MADE FROM PART OF A HANDKERCHIEF.

Almost inexhaustible are the possibilities of fine handkerchiefs. They may be worked successfully into bags, jabots, sofa pillows, aprons, lingerie, bureau scarfs, pin-cushions, and innumerable other articles.

The sofa pillow-cover illustrated is faintly reminiscent of the patchwork which captivated our grandmothers. For it are required two 12-inch handkerchiefs and one 6-inch handkerchief centre. The two larger handkerchiefs are cut diagonally in half, giving four pieces. On each piece the point formed by the uncut corner is turned back to a depth sufficient to form a triangular flap, with a base of 6 inches. These four pieces are then joined with insertion, making a square with a smaller square-opening in the centre, formed by the turning back of the corners. Into this opening the 6 inch handkerchief-centre is set and joined in place with insertion. With a plain handkerchief linen or mull back, this cover will look very dainty over a pink or blue foundation, and if the side left open for putting in the pillow is finished with a flap and small buttons and button-holes, it may be taken off and laundered easily.

A TABLE SCARF MADE OF FOUR GAILY PRINTED HANDKERCHIEFS WITH BLUE BORDERS.

The fine-work apron is made of cross-bar linen handkerchiefs, three being necessary. One handkerchief forms the centre of the apron. The other two are cut into halves and one of the halves into quarters. A half handkerchief forms the bottom and each of the sides, and the two quarters are used to fill in the corners. All are joined with lace insertion. A lace ruffle finishes the edge,

AN APRON OF CROSS-BARRED LINEN HANDKERCHIEFS.

and beading threaded with ribbon serves for the waistband.

A simple but very effective apron may be fashioned from two large fancy coloured handkerchiefs, one for the body of the apron and the other for the ruffle. The handkerchief which forms the apron proper should be cut out at one corner to fit smoothly about the waist. To make the ruffle, cut from the other handkerchief (supposing it to be 18 inches square, the usual size for these handkerchiefs) a pear-shaped piece about 16 inches long by 5 inches at its greatest width. This will give a circular ruffle to be fitted around the bottom of the apron. These coloured handkerchiefs cost only a few pence each, and work up very effectively. The gayer and brighter the pattern

CUSHION COVER MADE OF HANDKERCHIEFS.

## Trifles made from Handkerchiefs.

the better the results. They give an effect similar to cretonne, while the hemstitched edges save many tedious stitches.

A novel little bag a convenient size for holding crochet work can be evolved out of a small centre and two handkerchiefs of ordinary size. The centre is used for the bottom of the bag. The handker-

ANOTHER HANDKERCHIEF JABOT.

chiefs are cut diagonally in half, half forming each side of the bag. The raw edge, where the handkerchief was cut on the diagonal, is gathered in to fit one side of the bottom. The sides are over-handed together part way up, and the points at the top are turned down on the outside to form the mouth of the bag. A row of feather-stitch-ing will fasten them down in place and make a casing through which to run a ribbon draw-string. Now, last of all, take

A HANDKERCHIEF WORKBAG.

a piece of cardboard the size of the bottom of the bag, and, after padding with scented cotton, cover with a light silk. This tacked in the bottom of the bag will give it shape.

An attractive table-cover may be made from four or five such handkerchiefs, combined with coarse lace

insertion. The discarded corners of the two end handkerchiefs may be used in some other combination. Delightful bags and sofa pillows in all the conventional styles may also be made from these artistic offsprings of the bandanna.

Jabots are most simple in construction, and one may use handkerchiefs or the little centres, according to the size of jabot desired. A fine 7 or 8-inch handkerchief, trimmed with French Valenciennes or a baby Irish edge, and with the hem decorated with a row of French knots or satin-stitch dots worked in a colour, will make a small jabot that compares favourably with the more expensive neckwear that one can buy. All that is required to be done is to cut off one corner and pleat in to a bit of tape, pressing the pleats in shape. Numerous other styles will present themselves immediately to mind. The first jabot is made from a handkerchief 11 inches square. At one corner measure off and mark at 6 inches along each hem, fold across from mark to mark and cut along the fold.

This is the top of the jabot. Fold from the middle of this cut edge to the lowest point and cut along the fold. Finish these edges with lace, or, as in this case, bind them with washable ribbon. Sew lace to the hem edges and lay two pleats in the top of each piece, the pleats turning toward the longer edge. Lay one pleated piece over the other and bind the top with a piece of lawn. The cut-off corner may be pleated into a tiny jabot. The two other jabots are both cut from one linen handkerchief. There is a line of embroidery just inside the hem, and tiny sprays dotted over it—machine-embroidery, certainly, but no one would suspect that two such dainty jabots had been evolved from one handkerchief. For the diagonal jabot measure 7¼ inches on one hem and 4 inches on the hem opposite. Fold obliquely from one mark to the other and cut on the fold. Lay small close pleats along the cut edge. The other jabot measures 4¾ inches at each side hem (it was a 12-inch handkerchief), and is sloped to 3¾ inches at the centre, then pleated.

SOME DESIGNS FROM MEXICO FOR TENERIFFE WHEELS.

# Distinctive Touches in Hand Trimming.

It is the little touches of hand-made trimming that give individuality to an otherwise ordinary garment, and some of the stitches shown in our illustrations may serve as suggestions for the home worker to ornament her clothes.

Arrow-heads (or crow-toes, as they are sometimes called), that tailors work at the corners of pockets to strengthen, in an ornamental way,

1. AN ARROW-HEAD.

2. METHOD OF WORK-
ING ARROW-HEAD.

the places where strain comes, are also used in other ways where only the ornamental value is retained. One of these ways is to work them on a dress with mercerised embroidery cotton either the colour of the dress or in white. In illustrations I. and II. a completed arrow-head and the method of working are shown. This makes an attractive finish down the side-front closing of a simple frock. Black silk would be suitable for working on blue serge. White looks well on blue, or blue or pink on white. A large button, placed far enough from the wide end of the arrow-head to leave its outline clear, completes the finish.

The arrow-heads, to be effective, should be quite large—2½ inches long, perhaps, and about 1 inch wide at

the base. It will be advisable to mark out the arrow-head on a piece of stiff paper or light cardboard ; cut it out and use it as a pattern by laying it on the dress in the required position and marking round it with a lead-pencil. A piece of lining somewhat larger than the arrow-head should be basted underneath the cloth to give it greater firmness, and after the work is done the surplus lining may be trimmed away close to the stitchery.

The method of working is plainly shown in the illustration. The needle is brought up through the cloth at the point at the top, then passed in at the lower point at the right-hand side and out at the corresponding point at the left hand. The next stitch is taken in at the right hand just below the top point and out at the left, keeping on the pencilled outline. All the stitches on the underside will be straight across. On the upper side they weave, one over the other, in diagonal lines.

Tailors use small crow-toes as a finish for the rows of stitching that hold skirt pleats

DECORATIVE USE OF
WOODEN BUTTON MOULDS.

METHOD OF WORKING
FRENCH FAGGOTING

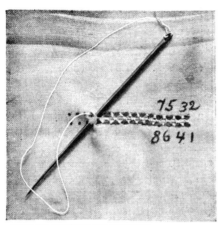

METHOD OF WORKING BERMUDA
FAGGOTING.

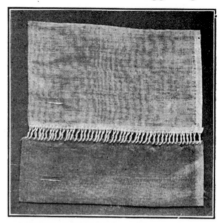

COLOURED HEM APPLIED WITH
FRENCH FAGGOTING.

in position, but made large they are a decidedly pretty and easily made trimming.

An attractive way to decorate a simple white crêpe blouse is to sew buttons on with colour-ed embroidery thread, the

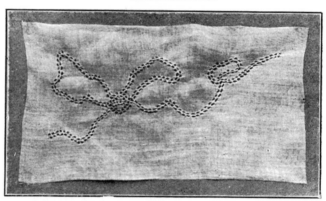

A FREEHAND DESIGN IN BERMUDA
FAGGOTING STITCH.

thread running from the holes over the edge of the buttons in-stead of from hole to hole, as shown in the illustra-tion. A dull blue shade of "Peri-Lusta" would look effective in this way. Put each little button at the end of a short line of chain-stitching done in the same blue thread and arrange in little groups on the blouse. A manner of using uncovered wooden button moulds is shown on page 22.

Coloured hems applied

CHAIN-STITCH AND SMALL
BUTTONS.

with French faggoting look well on the side frills now being worn. Two illustrations show the method of working, and completed effect of this work. It differs some-what from the ordinary faggoting in that the lines run straight from one edge to the other, and the effect is almost the same as hemstitching.

The two materials to be joined should be basted to a strip of stiff paper—the desired space between the two. In taking the stitch into the piece above the opening, bring the thread around in front of the needle, as if about to make a buttonhole. Take the stitch into the other piece of material without wrapping the thread around.

Bermuda faggoting is a good imitation of drawn-work, without however actually drawing any threads. A very coarse sewing-needle is used, and an end of the very finest linen thread is tied into the eye of the needle. The detail illustration on page 23 shows how the holes are consecutively made. The needle is brought up at 1, passed down again at 2, and the free end of the thread is tied on the wrong side; another stitch is taken from 2 to 1 and the thread is drawn tight; then the needle is put in at 2 and brought out at 3. Repeat this stitch from 2 to 3.

Now pass the needle in at 2 and out at 4, make a stitch from 1 to 4; repeat it, then a stitch and repeat from 3 to 4. This ties the first little group of 4 holes.

In all the straight passes of the needle, but not in the diagonals, the stitch is made twice to hold the little groups of threads securely. Now work from 3 to 5, pass from 3 to 6, work from 4 to 6, then from 5 to 6. Continue in this manner.

The beginner should make dots about one-eighth of an inch apart for her guidance, but presently will not find it necessary. Any design drawn on thin fabric may be worked out in this faggoting stitch. It is also useful in insetting lace or other inserts; one row of holes may be in the insert, the other in the body of the material.

# A Crochet Ring for Inlet.

Using Manlove's No. 60 Irish Lace Thread, commence with 10 ch, turn, 1 tr into the fourth ch, 3 ch 1 tr into the first ch, turn.

*1st Row.*—* 6 ch, 3 tr into first sp, 3 ch, 3 tr into next sp, turn.

*2nd Row.*—6 ch, 3 d c 5 ch 3 d c into next sp, 3 ch 1 tr into next sp, 3 ch 1 tr into same sp, turn.

*3rd Row.*—6 ch, 3 tr into first sp, 5 ch 3 tr into each of next 2 sp, 3 ch 3 tr into same sp as last tr, turn.

*4th Row.*— 6 ch, 3 d c 5 ch 3 d c into

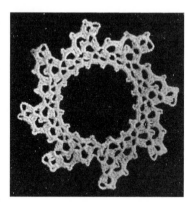

first sp, 1 d c into centre of next tr, 3 d c 5 ch 5 d c into next sp, 1 d c into centre of next tr, 3 d c 5 ch 3 d c into next sp, 3 ch 1 tr into next sp twice, turn and repeat from *, until there are eight finished points, then close the ring by slip-stitching through the last two sp on the last row and the foundation chain stitches for first 2 sp. Finish the inside of the ring by working a row of close d c into the loops, putting a 5 ch picot after each fifth d c.

# A D'oiley in Irish Braid Appliqué.

Among the latest novelties in table napery is this new Irish braid appliqué. The braids used in making Irish renaissance lace are appliquéd on net of various degrees of fineness, the braids matching the net in texture.

The design must first be drawn or traced on a piece of white drawing paper, then the lines gone over with pen and ink so that they may show clearly through the net which is next tacked over the design securely ; tack the piece of linen on the centre and cut away the surplus from the centre of the two inner lines. Now tack the braid between the two lines near its outer edge, interlacing them at the corners as in the illustration. The braid is now to be sewn over the edge to the net, and to the net and linen on the inner line, fulling the braid a little to make it fit the inner curves. Remove the lace from the design by cutting the threads on the back of the paper, cut away the superfluous net all round and sew on the pearl edging. Cut away the net from behind the linen centre.

The lace is now ready to be further adorned with any lace stitches with which the worker is familiar, or these may be omitted if liked ; however, the greater the amount of work put in, the more will be the value of the d'oiley. On another page we give a number of suggestions for filling-in stitches and darning on net.

# A Centre
# with Venetian Crochet.

THE COMPLETE CENTREPIECE.

A good linen to use for this Centre would be Robinson and Cleaver's "Grass-bleached" Linen No. ML 3. It is warranted pure flax, and the price ranges upward from 1/9½ per yard, 40 inches wide, to 2/6 per yard, 54 inches wide.

For the lace use Hicks, Bullick and Co.'s No. 42 Irish Lace Thread, this same firm's No. 10 for padding, and a No. 6 crochet hook.

**For the Insert.**

Join 6 ch in a ring; into this put 12 d c, 1 single through the first d c, 6 ch 1 tr into the third d c, 3 ch 1 tr into every second d c, 3 ch 1 single through the third of the first ch, making 6 sp.

*3rd Row.*—6 d c into each sp.

*4th Row.*—* 1 d c into first d c, 2 tr into next, 2 long tr into next, 6 ch, form into a picot over last tr, 2 long tr into next, 2 tr into next, 1 d c into next; repeat from * over each sp.

*5th Row.*—1 d c into first picot, 6 ch, 1 triple tr into the d c over the tr below, 6 ch 1 d c into next picot, repeat from *

*6th Row.*—10 d c into each sp.

26

*7th Row.*—* 10 d c into next 10 d c, 1 d c over the long tr, 10 d c into next 10, 10 ch, turn, miss next ch, 9 d c into 9 ch, work 2 rows of d c around this leaflet, then a row of d c with a 5 ch picot on the top and three at each side ; repeat from *.

*8th Row.*—* 1 d c into the picot on top of leaflet, 10 ch, 3 quadruple tr (thread four times over the needle) over the long tr, retaining the last loop in each until finishing the third, 10 ch ; repeat from *.

*9th Row.*—d c closely into each sp.

This motif is placed on the centre of the linen and the size marked, then a perfect circle is drawn there and outlined in button-hole stitch ; the centre is cut away and the motif sewn in place on the wrong side.

### The Motif for the Edge.

Make a padding cord of six strands of the coarse thread and form a d c in the folded end, twist the cord round to form a ring of double padding cord, work 40 d c into the ring, pull the end of the cord to make the ring compact. 1 single through the first d c, 4 d c into next 4, 20 ch, turn.

1 tr into the fourteenth ch, 2 ch 1 tr into every third ch, 2 ch 1 d c into the ring, turn.

3 d c into every sp at both sides and 9 d c into the top sp, turn.

1 d c into each up the side and to the centre top, 7 ch, turn.

A DETAIL OF THE CORNER.

## A Centre with Venetian Crochet.

Miss 2 ch, 1 d c into each 5 ch, and into each d c down the side, 1 d c into the ring, turn.

Work 3 more rows all round, then take up the padding and work d c over it into each d c all round.

Repeat the 4 d c into next on ring, then this leaflet again.

THE INSERT.

For the middle leaflet commence as in the last, work 10 rows of the d c at each side but narrowing off at the lower side by omitting the last stitch in every row, and turning back in the 5th and 8th rows when within 5 stitches from the top. Slip-stitch to the ring, and, taking up the padding, work the d c all round, then repeat the first two leaflets.

The stem is worked on a similar padding cord, d c over a length of 3½ inches, turn the cord round to form a loop ½-inch in diameter, secure in place with a d c, then continue working d c for another 1½ ins. Leave the cord and work 2 rows of d c, take up the cord and work d c over it into the last row, shaping the stem by gently pulling the cord into shape and secure the loop with another d c at this side.

The stem is now sewn to the flower after the manner illustrated, and the spaces filled in with a few bars of chain stitches with picots. The motifs are placed around the square of linen and the inner edge marked; outline this edge with button-hole stitch and top-sew the motifs in the proper position to the button-hole stitches.

The lower leaves are held in position with a bar of ch worked over with d c and a 5 ch picot formed in the centre.

A WORKING DETAIL OF THE BORDER.

# Ideas for Chemise Tops.

**Several of these Designs would be equally suitable for applying
to Camisoles, or to the Tops of Linen or Silk Overblouses.**

### A Chemise Top with a Bell Design.

Using Hicks, Bullick & Co's Shamrock Crochet Cotton No. 40, commence with the ring on the centre front, into which put 24 ch, 6 loops of 12 ch each with 6 d c

A CHEMISE TOP WITH
A BELL DESIGN.

between the loops, into the ring. Break off the thread and fasten to top of the first loop with a d c, 5 ch 1 d c into this loop 3 times.

*2nd Row.*—3 ch 1 d c into first loop, 5 ch 1 d c into same loop, 5 ch 1 d c into each of next 2 loops twice. Turn.

*3rd Row.*—* 3 ch 1 d c into first loop, 5 ch 1 d c into next loop, 5 ch, 5 d c into centre loop, 5 ch 1 d c into each of next 2 loops. Turn.

*4th Row.*—8 ch 1 d c into first loop, 5 ch 1 d c into next loop, 5 ch 1 d c into next loop, crossing over the d c bar, 5 ch 1 d c into each of next 2 loops, repeat from * until 7 d c bars are formed.

On the rows of 2 loops at each side of the d c bars form 2 long strips of

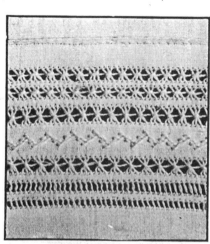

The drawn-thread work is the feature of the
straight yoke of which this is a section.

the same pattern commenced in the same way, each strip containing 27 bars. Work another in the pattern, and on this form a row of the loops over the bars with the loops at each side and the bars at each side of the centre row of loops, after the fifth bar. Break off the thread and finish the other strip in the same way.

Turn, work to end of row and take up the first strip and work over it, preserving the pattern, making 6 bars at the lower end and increasing the number of d c by 1 in each row, put 7 bars in the next row of bars, then 8 and finally 9 bars in the top row.

Over the top row of loops form another strip of the loops and bars, and continue this

## Ideas for Chemise Tops.

round for the length of the neck to the centre back.

Commence the other side on the last loop in the centre ring, working so that the d c are upon the right side throughout.

To connect the 2 strips by filling

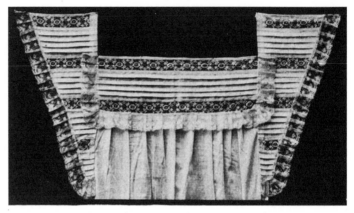

This simple yet pretty design is nothing but straight tucks and insertion.

in the centre, commence at the outside angle and work d c into the first 3 sp, next sp 2 d c 5 ch 2 d c, next 3 d c, next 2 d c 5 ch 2 d c, 3 d c into next sp, into the loop after the 27th bar put * 5 ch, 2 tr 5 ch 2 long tr 5 ch 2 tr, 5 ch 3 d c into second next sp, 5 ch * and repeat into every second loop for 4 more groups of tr, 3 d c into each of next 2 bars, 2 d c 5 ch 2 d c into next sp, 3 d c into next, 2 d c 5 ch 2 d c into next, then 3 d c into each to the

angle. Continue working along the under side of the top strip to correspond with the last.

Break off the thread and fasten to the last picot formed, 3 ch, cross over to the opposite picot and put 1 d c into it, 7 ch 2 tr into next picot, * 2 tr into next sp, 3 ch 3 tr into each of next 2 sp, 3 ch 2 tr into next sp, and repeat 4 times, 7 ch into next picot, 5 ch into same picot, 7 ch 1 d c into next picot.

Cross over to the picot on opposite strip and make a d c into it, 7 ch 1 d c into next picot, 7 ch into next picot, 2 ch 1 d c into the picot at opposite side, 2 ch 1 d c into last picot close beside the first d c into that picot,

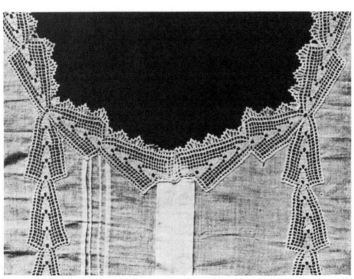

A CHEMISE TOP THAT CAN OPEN IN FRONT.

The Crochet is carried right round the top of the garment.

7 ch * 2 tr into next sp, 5 dc into next sp, 2 ch, cross over to the centre loop on the group at the opposite side and put 1 d c into it, 2 ch, 5 d c over next bar on upper edge, 2 tr into next sp, and repeat from *, ending with 7 ch into the last picot.

## A Top with Honiton Braid.

A TOP WITH HONITON BRAID.

**For the Top Edging.**

Commence at the back.

*1st Row.*—* 2 long tr into first loop, 3 ch 2 long tr into each of next 2 loops,

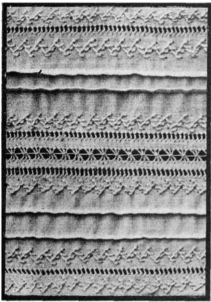

· A section of another straight yoke.
The disposition of the featherstitching, the tucks and the drawn-thread work, make this a handsome design.

5 ch 2 long tr into next loop but one, 5 ch miss next loop and repeat from *, putting 2 long tr 3 ch 2 long tr into the centre ring.

*2nd Row.*—* 3 d c into first sp, 3 ch 3 d c into next sp, 7 ch, 1 tr into the stitch before next trs, into each tr and into the following stitch, 7 ch and repeat from *.

*3rd Row.*—* 2 d c over the 3 ch, 7 ch, 3 tr before the trs and 1 tr into first tr, 3 ch, 1 tr into last tr and 3 tr after it, 7 ch and repeat from *.

*4th Row.*—* 1 d c over the 7 ch, 6 long tr into the sp between the 4 tr with 2 ch between them, 5 ch 2 d c into next sp, 3 ch and repeat from *.

*5th Row.*—5 ch loops into each sp with 2 d c between and 4 d c over the ch's between the mitres.

The four lower figures are worked in the pattern exactly as in the end of the 2 long strips, having 6 and 7 d c bars in the lower figure, and 8 and 9 in the upper at each side.

31

## Ideas for Chemise Tops.

### A Chemise Top that can Open in Front.

For this use Barbour's F.D.A. Linen Thread No. 36.

The crochet is carried right round the top of the chemise. It can be made to open in front, with tucks, gathers, or the material plain, as best suits the wearer.

Commence at the right front strip of insertion, 14 ch, join in a ring into which put 1 tr 3 ch 4 tr 3 ch 1 tr, turn.

*2nd Row.*—6 ch 2 tr into first tr, 1 tr into each of next 2 tr, 2 tr into last tr, 3 ch 1 tr into top of last tr, turn.

*3rd Row.*—6 ch, 2 tr into first and last tr and 1 tr into the intervening tr, 3 ch 1 tr into the fourth ch at the turning.

*4th Row.*—6 ch, 2 tr into first and last and 1 tr into each intervening, 3 ch 1 tr into the fourth ch.

*5th Row.*—6 ch, 2 tr into first tr, 1 tr into each of next 2, 4 ch, miss 6 tr, 1 tr into each of next 2, 2 tr into last tr, 3 ch 1 tr into fourth ch.

*6th Row.*—6 ch 1 tr into first tr, 3 ch 4 tr into centre, 3 ch 1 tr into fourth tr, 3 ch 1 tr into 4th ch.

*7th Row.*—Repeat from 2nd Row, having 2 sp at each side of the tr, then onwards increasing the number of sp at the sides of the tr by 1 for each group of tr. This section repeated forms the pattern. After the fourth group of tr is completed, break off the thread and commence another section on the centre loop. Work a strip long enough to go round one half the neck portion.

Commencing at the other side of the ring work two sections to reach the centre front. From the ring again work a third strip for the insertion of three sections.

Work a row of d c all round the sp, putting 3 d c into each and 6 d c into every corner. Then work a second

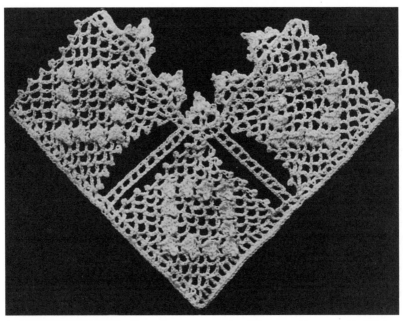

A PRETTY INSERTION FOR THE TOP OF A CHEMISE, WITH
BARS FOR RUNNING IN BROAD RIBBON.

32

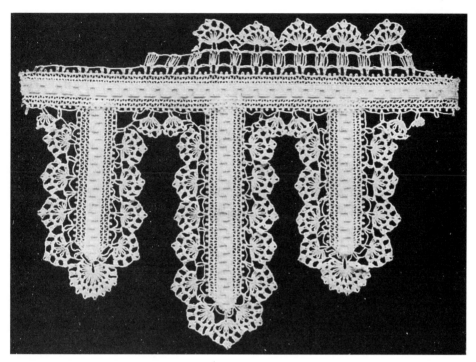

A LACY FRONT ON FANCY BRAID.

row of sp, 3 ch 1 tr into each tr, with 6 ch and a second tr into each corner. Finish with a row of d c as before.

### For the Edging.

1 d c into first corner stitch, * 3 ch 2 tr into next tr, 3 ch 2 long tr into next tr, 3 ch 2 triple tr into next tr, 5 ch 2 triple tr into same tr as last, 3 ch 2 long tr into next tr, 3 ch 2 tr into next tr, 3 ch 1 d c into next, repeat from * twice, then work d c into those between this point and the top of next section, where you repeat from the first.

*2nd Row.*—2 d c 5 ch 2 d c into each sp between the tr, 2 d c into the sp at each side of the d c. After working into the last sp on a section, cross over to the corresponding stitch on the next and put a d c into each until within 3 d c from the next point, 5 ch, fasten these back to last picot, turn, and put 3 d c 5 ch 3 d c over it, then continue and repeat from the first.

### Honiton Braid and Crochet Chemise Front.

This would also look well for the top of a fine overblouse.

Use Manlove's No. 42 cotton.

Cut a length of 25 ovals from a piece of Honiton braid same pattern as in the illustration. Fasten the cotton to the end of the first oval and neaten it with 2 d c, * 9 ch, 2 tr into end of oval, 2 ch, 2 tr into centre of oval, 2 ch 2 tr into end of oval, 9 ch 2 d c over the bar between the ovals, * repeat at both sides of the braid.

*2nd Row.*—* 2 tr into the top of the 9 ch, 7 ch, 2 tr into first 2 ch sp, 2 ch 2 tr into next sp, 7 ch, 2 tr over top of 9 ch, repeat from * at both sides.

## Ideas for Chemise Tops.

Finish the 2 loops at each side of the end with 9 tr.

*3rd Top Row.*

—* 7 ch 2 tr into the 2 ch sp, 7 ch 2 long tr into the sp between the ovals, repeat from * along the top, then finish this side

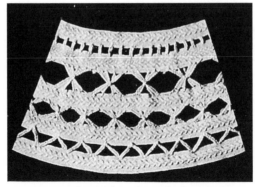

A section of a circular yoke made from Cash's Featherstitched Trimming and united by hand work.

with 3 d c 5 ch 3 d c into each sp, finishing each end with 5 ch 2 d c into the centre of the 9 tr, 5 ch 2 d c into the d c over the end of the braid.

For the centre-piece cut off 17 ovals, turn the fifth, sixth, and seventh ovals round to form the lower figure, crossing at the bar between the fourth and fifth ovals, secure with a few tight stitches and sew the two ends of the braid together, join the first and last ovals

at the inner side with a d c near the end, * 7 ch 2 ch over next bar, at the top side, 7 ch 3 d c into end of next oval, 5 ch 3 d c into other side of the oval, and repeat from *. Continue along the other side with 4 d c into end of first oval, * 7 ch 4 tr over next bar, 7 ch 4 d c into beginning of next oval, 5 ch 4 d c into end of same oval, and repeat from *.

5 d c 5 ch 5 d c over first bar at the top side, * 3 d c into the stitches over the bars, 5 d c 5 ch 5 d c over next bar, 4 d c into next 4 d c, 5 d c into the loop catching in the picot at the opposite side in the centre d c, 5 d c 5 ch 5 d c over next chs, and repeat from *.

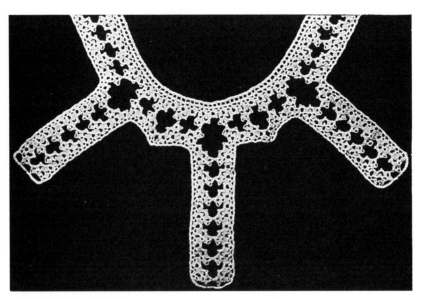

FOR RIBBON WITH THREE NARROW PANELS.

Break off the thread and fasten it to the end over the joining with 3 d c, * 9 ch, four groups of 2 tr each into oval with 2 ch between 9 ch 1 d c over next bar, repeat from * down to the oval before the three lower ovals, into which put only two groups of tr, 2 ch 2 tr into next, twice, continue the

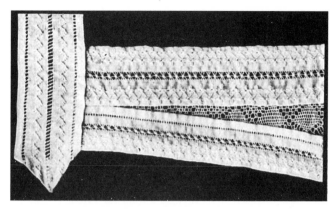

One half of a yoke and sleeve, made from two straight bands of worked material. The lower band is brought to a point in the centre and mitred, the intervening space being filled with torchon.

pattern into the lower oval, work up the side as opposite, then continue on to the end.

*2nd Row.*—3 d c into the 3 d c on the end, into next sp 3 d c, 7 ch 5 long tr 7 ch 3 d c, * 7 ch 2 tr into first 2 ch sp, 2 ch, 2 tr into each of next 2 sp, 7 ch 2 tr into next, 2 tr into next and repeat from *. Over the

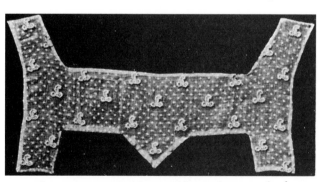

A lawn yoke covered with French dots, and a conventional motif in raised embroidery.

2 centre ovals omit the 2 ch between the two groups and the two groups below. Into the two end loops put the d c's and long trs as at the first loop in this row, and into the 2 loops at each side of the lower oval. Work the remaining portion in the pattern.

*3rd Top Row.*—Fasten the thread

with 2 tr into the first 2 ch sp on first oval, 1 ch 1 d c into the 2 ch on the oval above in the first strip, 1 ch 2 tr into next sp of row, 7 ch 1 d c between the two groups of tr between the ovals, 7 ch and repeat the trs and the chs into last row, ending by joining to top row between last two groups. Break off the thread and fasten it to the next oval on the top strip with 2 d c over the 2 ch, * 3 long tr into next loop on centrepiece, 7 ch 2 d c over third tr, 7 ch 3 long tr over next loop, repeat from *. 7 ch, 2 tr into first 2 ch sp, 2 ch 2 tr into next sp, 7 ch, 1 d c between the centre trs, then repeat over each oval, putting the long trs as at the beginning of the row over those at each side of the lower end. Working the trs into the remaining stitches at the right side, ending at the point opposite where the row began.

*4th Row.*—Around the centre-piece

## Ideas for
## Chemise Tops.

fasten the thread to the end of the oval on the top strip before the centre-piece, 2 d c 3 long tr with 7 ch between into last sp, 3 long tr into next sp on next oval, * 3 long tr into each of next 2 loops on centre-piece, 7 ch 1 d c between next trs, and repeat from * into next, 7 ch 5 long tr into next sp, 7 ch 1 d c between next trs, * 7 ch 3 long tr into next loop, 3 long tr into next loop, 7 ch 1 d c between next trs, repeat from * over next 4 ovals and put the 5 long tr at each side of the centre front, then work the other side in the same way.

Fasten the thread to the end of the top piece after the 9 tr, with 1 d c, * 7 ch, into the sp between the trs put 3 long tr 5 ch 3 long tr, 7 ch 1 d c between two centre groups of tr, and repeat from *. Put long trs into the long trs of last row, and 5 d c over each 7 ch between the groups. End at the corresponding point on the other side of the top strip.

## A Very Handsome
## Chemise Front.

In this top there has been more work put in at one side of the centre than the other, so that any who might think the 2 motifs at the side of the centre front sufficient could make it that way. For those who would like a little more at the top of the front, a second motif like the first has been added and a third smaller at the corner of the front section.

Use Ardern's No. 22 Crochet Cotton to make a length of ch stitches to go around the top of the space the work is to fill.

With Ardern's No. 42 Crochet Cotton put * 5 ch 1 d c into every second ch 3 times, 5 ch, miss 3, 1 d c into next ch, * and repeat, taking care

to have 3 loops on the centre of the ch and an equal number of 5 ch bars at each side of the centre.

*2nd Row.*—Turn with 6 ch 1 d c into first loop, 5 ch 1 d c into each of next 2, 5 d c over the 5 ch and repeat the 5 ch into each loop, with the d c over the 5 ch bars.

*3rd Row.*—Repeat the first, putting the 5 ch over the d c and a second loop into the centre of the middle 3.

In the centre loop is made the increase in every row, but when there are sufficient loops at each side of this the pattern is carried out. When 4 bars at each end are completed, break off the thread and fasten to the end of the second bar and continue to the corresponding stitch at the opposite end until 2 more bars are formed, again break off the thread and fasten to the end of the fourth line of bars, repeat the pattern until there are 8 lines of bars, then break off as before, and after 10 bars are complete pass over 4 lines and work 2 more bars on next strip, 2 more on next, 6 on next, and so on down to the point.

For the narrow insertion at the top work a long strip the length of the foundation ch of 4 loops of 5 ch each.

For the edging, * 3 d c into first sp, 2 d c into next, 18 ch 2 d c into same sp, repeat from *, then work a second row of 3 tr 7 ch 1 d c 7 ch 3 tr into each loop.

Sew this insertion at the top.

The motif at each side of the front is next formed. Into the 3 corner loops of the strip, having 12 bars at one side and 10 at the other, put 3 of the 5 ch loops with 3 ch between for the bars, turn with 6 ch and work until 6 bars are formed, increasing in each row the number of ch and d c by 1, then again work 3 of these motifs in the same way from each of the 3 loops. In the last row connect at the end to both sides of the upper part. The second motif at each side is worked in the same way, and the third at the top has only the first half of the last.

The sleeves may be finished with a strip of the insertion as at the neck portion.

## A Design with Bars for Running in Broad Ribbon.

This pattern is worked in Manlove's No. 36 Thread, and will take ribbon 1¼-inches wide.

*1st Row.*—38 ch.

*2nd Row.*—1 tr into fourth ch from needle, * 2 ch, miss 2 ch, 1 tr into next, repeat from * 9 times ; 1 ch, miss 1 ch, 1 tr into next. This makes bar for ribbon to go *over.* Turn.

*3rd Row.*—3 ch, miss 1 tr, 1 tr into next tr, * 8 ch, 1 s c into fifth ch from needle (this forms picot), repeat from * till 7 picots with 3 ch between each are formed ; 3 ch, 1 tr on tr of previous

A VERY HANDSOME FRONT·

row, 1 ch, 1 tr on second ch of last row.

*4th Row.*—3 ch, miss 1 tr, make 1 tr into next tr, 3 ch, 1 d c over ch before picot, 5 ch, 1 d c between each picot. (Keep the picots pointing to the last row). Make 7 loops of 5 ch, 1 d c, 3 ch, 1 tr into tr of last row, 1 ch, miss 1 ch, 1 tr into next.

*5th Row.*—5 ch, 1 d c into second tr from needle, * 5 ch, 1 d c over loop of 5 ch in last row, repeat twice from *, 3 ch, 1 d c, 2 tr, 1 picot (5 ch, 1 s c into last tr), 2 tr, 1 d c over next loop (this makes a group), 3 ch, 1 d c over next loop, 5 ch, 1 d c over next loop, 5 ch, 1 d c over next loop, 5 ch. 1 d c into tr, 3 ch, miss 1 ch, 1 tr into next.

*6th Row.*—3 ch, 1 tr into d c of last row, 3 ch, 1 d c over first loop, 5 ch, 1 d c over each loop of 5 ch, and over each loop of 3 ch on either side of group, making 7 loops of 5 ch ; then 3 ch, 1 tr into second ch at end of last row, 1 ch, miss 1 ch, 1 tr into next ch. This ought to give the effect of 2 tr, with 1 ch between, at the beginning and end of each row.

*7th Row.*—5 ch, miss 1 tr, 1 d c into next tr, 5 ch, 1 d c over first loop of 5 ch of last row, 5 ch, 1 d c over next loop, 3 ch, 1 group over next loop, 3 ch, 1 d c over next loop, 3 ch, 1 group over next loop, 3 ch, 1 d c over next loop, 5 ch, 1 d c over next loop, 5 ch, 1 d c into tr, 3 ch, miss 1 ch, 1 tr into next.

*8th Row.*—Same as 6th Row.

*9th Row.*—5 ch, 1 d c into second tr from needle, 5 ch, 1 d c over first loop, 3 ch, 1 group over next loop, 3 ch, 1 d c over next loop, * 5 ch, 1 d c over next loop, repeat once from * ; 3 ch, 1 group over next loop, 3 ch, 1 d c over next loop, 5 ch, 1 d c into tr

of last row, 3 ch, miss 1 ch, 1 tr into next ch.

*10th Row.*—Same as 6th row.

*11th Row.*—5 ch, 1 d c into second tr from needle, 3 ch, one group over next loop, 3 ch, 1 d c over next group, * 5 ch, 1 d c over next loop, repeat from * three times, 3 ch, one group over next loop, 3 ch, 1 d c into tr of last row, 3 ch, miss 1 ch, 1 tr into next.

*12th Row.*—Same as 6th.

*13th Row.*—Same as 9th.

*14th Row.*—Same as 6th.

*15th Row.*—Same as 7th.

*16th Row.*—Same as 6th.

*17th Row.*—Same as 5th.

*18th Row.*—Same as 6th.

*19th Row.*—5 ch, 1 d c into second tr from needle, * 7 ch, 1 s c into fifth ch from needle (forming picot), 2 ch, 1 d c over first loop from needle, repeat from * to end of row, making 8 picots in all, finishing with 1 d c in tr of last row, 3 ch, miss 1 ch, 1 tr on next ch. This makes motif for ribbon to go *under*.

*20th Row.*—3 ch, miss 1 ch, 1 tr into d c of last row, 30 ch, miss all the loops and make 1 tr into third ch, miss 1 ch, 1 tr into next.

*21st Row.*—3 ch, miss 1 tr, make 1 tr into next, * 2 ch, miss 2 ch, 1 tr into next, repeat from * 9 times, 1 ch, miss 1 ch, 1 tr on tr of last row. Repeat from 3rd row.

**Heading.**

Work 2 d c over side of each tr along the edge. After working * 9 d c, make 5 ch, then 4 more d c over edge. Turn. 4 ch, 1 d c, 5 ch, 1 d c over loop of 5 ch, 4 ch, 1 d c into fourth d c from needle. Turn. 2 d c, 5 ch, 2 d c over loop of 4 ch, 5 ch, 1 d c, 2 tr, 1 picot (5 ch, 1 s c into last tr), 2 tr, 1 d c over loop of 5 ch, 5 ch,

2 d c, 5 ch, 2 d c over loop of 4 ch. Repeat from *.

**Footing.**

2 d c into side of each tr at edge.

**For Corner.**

Begin motif as usual, but at end of 5th row omit 3 ch, miss 1 ch, 1 tr.

6*th* Row.—7 ch, 1 s c into fifth ch from needle (forming picot), 5 ch, 1 d c over each loop as usual in this row.

7*th* Row.—Proceed as' usual, but work 5 ch, 1 d c over loop before picot at end of row.

8*th* Row.— Same as 6th row for corner.

9*th* Row.— Proceed as usual for this

18*th* Row.—Same as 6th corner row.

19*th* Row.—3 ch, 1 tr into second tr from needle, * 1 ch, 1 long tr into first d c from needle, 1 ch, 1 tr into centre ch of loop, repeat from * to end of row, 3 ch, 1 tr into same place as last tr, 30 ch, 1 tr into tr at end of 5th row, 1 ch, 1 tr into tr of 3rd row. This turns the corner, and makes foundation chain for bar.

### A Lacy Front on a Fancy Braid.

Use Manlove's No. 42 Lace Thread.

Take a straight piece of fancy braid of the length required to fasten at back or on the shoulder. To this sew a strip

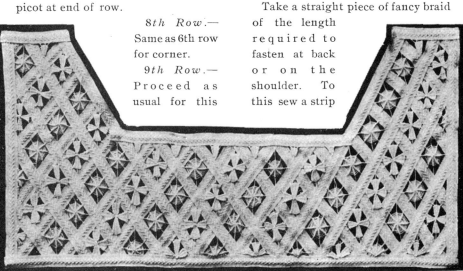

A Straight Yoke made from Cash's Featherstitched Trimming
united by Maltese crosses and wheels.

row, but work 5 ch, 1 d c over loop before picot. Turn.

10*th* Row.—Same as 6th corner row.

11*th* Row.—Proceed as usual, but after last group work 3 ch, 1 d c over loop before picot. Turn.

12*th* Row.—Same as 6th corner row.

13*th* Row.—Same as 9th corner row.

14*th* Row.—Same as 6th corner row.

15*th* Row.—Same as 7th corner row.

16*th* Row.—Same as 6th corner row.

17*th* Row.—Same as 5th corner row, finishing with 5 ch, 1 d c over loop before picot. Turn.

of braid to the centre for the front tab, and then another strip on each side, leaving 16 of the picot loops on the braid between each. The centre tab should have about 33 loops on each side, and the side tabs about 25 loops. But to save difficulties, do not mitre the braid till the crochet edge is done, only fold it back.

Starting at the lower edge. Make a loop of 12 ch into first picot loop on braid, then ch 12 and catch into fourth picot loop, in this make another long loop of 12 ch, and go all round the

## Ideas for Chemise Tops.

edge in the same way. At the bottom of each tab make a long loop of 12 ch right at the tip, and 1 on each side at the slope of the braid.

Into every alternate loop of 12 ch make 6 loops of 12 ch each.

Catch across the tops of the loops with 5 ch, and these are next filled in with 3 d c

A SUGGESTION FOR TRIMMING A CHILD'S DRESS WITH CROSS-STITCH BANDS.

5 ch 3 d c. From the last loop make 3 ch and 2 d c to catch into the alternate long loop below that does not contain a group of loops. The 10 ch carries you to the next long loop into which 6 loops are made as before.

Into the long loop at the tip of each tab make 10 loops instead of 6.

Now into each of the loops of 5 ch (that comes between the d c) make 3 tr, 3 ch to next, 3 tr, 3 ch to the middle loop, into this make 3 tr 3 ch 3 tr. And so on all round. At the bottom of each tab it will be seen that 3 tr 3 ch 3 tr occurs seven times to give the fan-like spread at the bottom.

### For the Upper Edging at the Neck.

Make * 1 tr into first picot loop, 3 ch, 1 tr into second loop, 9 ch, then miss 2 picots and repeat from *.

In the next row, make 3 loops of 18 ch, each with 2 d c between, above the 2 tr in row below. Then 2 d c, 4 ch 2 d c over the 9 ch below.

Into the top of each long loop put 2 d c with 2 ch between each loop, and 9 ch between each set of loops.

2 d c in first 2 ch below, then make a loop of 12 ch, 2 d c in second 2 ch below, 2 d c in nearest part of the 9 ch, 4 ch, 2 d c in other end of the 9 ch, 2 d c in next 2 ch below, then 4

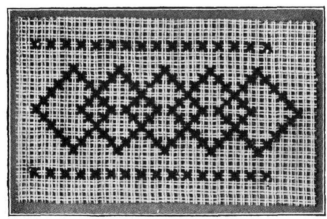

A WORKING DETAIL OF THE ABOVE DESIGN.

40

ch and 2 d c in next 2 ch below. Repeat, making the long loop alternate with the 4 ch. Then into each long loop of 12 ch make a group of 6 loops of 12 ch as in the lower edge.

Complete the scallops as for the lower edge.

## A Top for Ribbon with Three Narrow Panels.

Though this may look a little elaborate, it is practically 2 rows of edging caught together at the points ; the lower edge being so shaped, and worked in sections, as to make the front panels.

Use Manlove's No. 42 or No. 36 Irish Linen Thread.

Ch 6. Join in a ring. 6 ch, make 3 tr 3 ch 3 tr into ring.

* Turn with 6 ch, into first sp make 2 d c 4 ch 2 d c, into second sp make 1 tr 3 ch 1 tr.

6 ch, into first sp 3 tr 4 ch, in next sp 3 tr 4 ch, in top sp 3 tr 4 ch 3 tr.

6 ch, into first, second and third sp make 3 d c 4 ch 3 d c 3 ch, into last sp 1 tr 3 ch 1 tr.

6 ch, into first sp 3 tr 3 ch, into next sp 3 tr. Repeat from *.

Fill in each sp at the sewing-on edge with 3 d c. A ch should go along the end of each panel, filled in with d c.

For the top of the neck, after fitting in each sp with d c, work another row on top of these of 3 ch 1 tr all the way round. These sp in turn are to be filled with d c. The upper portion is done in one long strip to reach all round the neck. The lower portion is done in sections, to allow

of the points turning one way or the other as needed to match the points opposite.

Fancy crochet wheels could be let in between the panels.

## The Straight Yoke.

The Straight Yoke, which figures more than once in these designs, has much to recommend it. First, it is exceedingly simple in cut ; and second, if the shoulder-straps are not too long, it fits up over the chest, giving protection where it is needed.

As these yokes can be worked separately, they make excellent bits of fancy work for the drawing-room when one could not have the whole garment in hand.

Also, being hand-done on good material (and it is not worth while to put such work into poor stuff), these yokes will stand laundering better than the flimsy bought laces, and they give a girl's clothes some individuality, even though they are among the unseen things of one's wardrobe.

The illustration on page 39 shows a very novel straight yoke, made from Cash's insertion, united by lace stitches. The strips of insertion must be tacked down on to a stiff paper pattern, the cross-pieces being sewn to the edge, and the corners neatly but firmly sewn together. The Maltese crosses and wheels are then made in the spaces with linen lace thread. These will unite the yoke as a whole, but a few stitches at the places where the insertion strips cross will strengthen the work considerably.

# Lace Candle Shades.

Of the many varieties of lamp and candle shades, the most beautiful and artistic are those made of lace over a foundation of bright colour silk. The shape is first cut from a piece of stout

AN EMPIRE DESIGN IN LIMERICK TAMBOUR LACE.

parchment paper, or drawing paper answers very well. A pair of compasses will be useful to form the circles, as all the round shapes are composed of a segment of a circular piece. If the diameter at the top opening is to be two and a quarter inches (as in the shades shown here), two and a quarter inches will be the radius of the circle from which two of these shades can be cut. Draw the inner circle, then another 3 inches from the first for the outer edge. Cut out the circular piece, and divide into two equal parts. To prevent the shade from flaring out too much, a slanting piece can be cut away from the sides from the upper

corner to about an inch from the corner at the edge. Over this the silk is fastened with a small portion of seccotine along the edges, the shade is then fastened at the side with small paper-fasteners, and is ready to receive the lace, which is tacked neatly along the edges so that it can readily be removed when necessary to be laundered.

## An Empire Design in Limerick Tambour Lace.

This will look charming if made up over a rose-colour foundation, or any other brilliant colour to set off the design.

This tambour lace is quite easily made, and the stitch used is only the ordinary ch stitch used in crochet, and worked in the same way.

Cut out the shape in white paper, on which draw the design, tack a piece

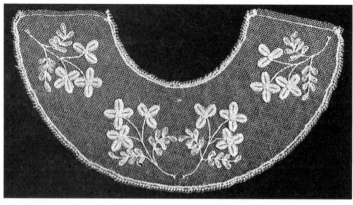

PRINCESS APPLIQUÉ ON NET.

42

of Brussels net over the paper, then with an ordinary sewing needle trace the design by running a fine thread in and out through the meshes over the lines ; now remove the net from the paper, and with No. 60 Barbour's Thread and a fine hook proceed to do the tambour work. Arrange the net in a small embroidery frame, make a loop on the end of the crochet thread with the hook, withdraw the hook, and take the loop in the left hand and hold it up under the frame close to the spot where you are to commence, settle the thread on the fingers as in crochet-work, with the

A SHADE IN IRISH CROCHET.

hook in the right hand, pull up the loop through the mesh, and make a ch stitch by hooking the thread through the next mesh over the tracing-line, and through the loop on the needle.

Proceed in this way all over the lines, working a row up and down inside each leaf, and filling up the spaces within the outlines of each figure. Work a row of chain stitches at each edge, which is afterwards finished off with a row of pearl edging whipped along the edge. This pearl edging can be bought at any fancy-work depot, and is usually

applied to all Limerick lace as a finish for the edge.

The lace is next pressed in the usual way, and the sides sewn neatly together.

### A Shade in Princess Appliqué on Fine Net.

The flowers are formed of 4 loops of lace braid with a group of French knots in the centre of each ; the stems and leaflets are worked with Ardern's No. 24 Lustrous Crochet Cotton ; the stems in twist stitch, and the leaflets in darning. The design is first copied as in the tambour lace, and the net tacked over it, then the braid is applied and sewn all round with neat even stitches, using very fine thread for the purpose.

Finish the edges with the pearl edging as directed for the tambour work.

### A Shade in Irish Crochet

Perhaps the most beautiful of all shades are those made of Irish crochet, as they certainly are the most durable. The shade illustrated has four motifs worked over a four-strand padding cord with No. 60 Irish lace thread and a fine crochet-hook.

Commence at the end of the stem of the trefoil and work d c over the padding for a length of 2 inches, then form the trefoil with 2 rows of tr and a row of d c all round, over the centre form a ring of d c over padding in the usual way. Work back on the stem to next figure, in which there are 2 rows of open work loops, each consisting of 3 ch.

## Lace Candle Shades.

The remainder is done in d c and tr; it can readily be copied by anyone familiar with Irish crochet. These motifs are tacked on the shape cut from a piece of paper, and they are then connected with large picot filling, in which each picot contains 10 ch, and each bar after the picot 5 ch. The usual straightening lines are worked at each side, and a picot edging finishes it.

# A Fancy Bag in Metallic Thread Crochet.

This bag can be made in a very short time from a few skeins of silver thread and a No. 4 crochet hook.

Ch 151, turn, 1 single through the 141st, 140th, and 139th ch, * 7 ch, miss 7, 3 single into next 3 ch, repeat from * 4 times more, 7 ch, miss 7, 5 single into next 5 ch, 11 ch, miss 11, 1 single into next, 11 ch, miss 11, 5 single into next 5, 11 ch, miss 11, 1 single

into next, 11 ch, miss 11, 1 single into next, 11 ch, miss 11, 1 single into next, 10 ch.

Turn, miss 2, 5 single into next 5, * 7 ch, 1 single into the 4th after the single in the last row, 4 single into next 4 ch, repeat from * twice, 11 ch, 5 single into the 5 on centre of next ch loop, 7 ch, 5 single into 5 on centre of next ch loop, 11 ch, 3 single on

centre of next loop, 7 ch 3 single on centre of each loop to the end.

Turn with 10 ch and repeat from the beginning.

There are 36 meshes around the bag, and the sides are joined with the single stitches in the last row, put into opposite loops at both sides together.

Join the lower end with a row of d c on the wrong side. Connect the little bars at the top with 4 ch 1 d c into the top of each, then form a heading of 5 ch 1 d c at each side the d c in the last row, fastening off the thread securely.

Line the bag with light silk, and add drawstrings made of a double ch with Peri-Lusta Esplen D'or Rope Embroidery Thread in colour to match the lining. Finish the ends of the strings with tassels.

# Afternoon Tea Serviettes.

Afternoon Tea Serviettes are useful as a protection for the dress. A serviette, folded in four, is handed to each person with the cup and saucer.

The serviette is usually of fine linen, or damask, from 12 to 15 inches square. One corner is generally ornamented with a design in embroidery or other fancy work, and the edge is finished in some artistic way suited to the purpose. Here is a work in which every girl has unlimited scope for showing her ingenuity and taste combined with skill in workmanship.

Crochet edgings, insertion, corners, monograms, openwork and embroidery are all suitable; sometimes colours are used with good effect when the shades employed match the design on the tea-service.

In the first of the serviettes illustrated we show a design having a deep hemstitched edge, with a row of openwork set one-and-a-quarter inches from it, on the four sides. One corner is ornamented with a small motif in Irish Crochet.

Cut out the square of linen to the required size, allowing one inch over for the hem. Draw 10 threads two inches from the outside on the four sides, then one-and-a-half inches from these draw the threads for the open-work of half-an-inch. Work the inner lines before turning in the hem by hemstitching at both sides of the drawn threads, taking in 6 threads with each stitch, and taking the same threads at both sides.

Form the wheel in the corner sp while doing the running through the centre. For this, fasten the thread with a knot around the centre of the second group of 6 threads from one end, pass the needle from right to left under these 6 threads and over the first 6, twist the needle round with the point towards you, at the same time bringing it up where it goes in before the second 6, draw out the needle and pull the stitch up evenly but not tight; now insert the needle from right to left under the second next group, put the point in where the last stitch came out, and twist it round towards you, bringing up the first group of 6 threads, pull the needle through and draw up the stitch as before. Repeat with every two groups of thread.

45

A MOTIF IN CUT-WORK.

point of a pencil or the top of a steel crochet-hook—to form a thick padded ring. Into this put 32 d s, close the ring with a single through the first d c, * 8 ch 1 d c into each of the first 8 d c, turn, 4 ch 1 d c into last loop, 5 ch 1 d c into each loop, 2 ch 1 d c into last loop and 5 ch into each loop in each of following rows until only one loop remains in the row ; break off the thread and repeat from * 3 times more.

Now take a small length of a padding-cord made from eight strands of the thread, and fasten with a d c to the beginning of the first row in the first petal ; work d c closely over the cord all round each petal, putting a 5 ch picot after each fifth d c. Fasten the cord securely on the back and cut away the superfluous thread. Make 4 ch to reach the first picot and put a d c through it and the picot at the opposite side together, 4 ch 1 d c into each picot all round and taking up

The wheel is formed while doing the second row at the crossing. Bring the thread as far as the centre of the sp and secure to the first with a knot-stitch, then take a long stitch to each corner, twisting the thread around the first stitch 3 times to reach the centre again, then work in and out through these bars around the centre for about 6 rows. Secure the end of the thread on the back and continue the open-work to the end.

Now turn in the edge of the hem very evenly and turn the edge to the line of drawn-threads, tack in place securely and hemstitch all round the serviette. Work the other side of the drawn-threads also, and form a tiny wheel in the sp where the lines cross.

### For the Corner Motif.

Use Hicks, Bullick & Co.'s No. 40 Shamrock Crochet Cotton, and wind the end of the thread several times around a very small mesh—such as the

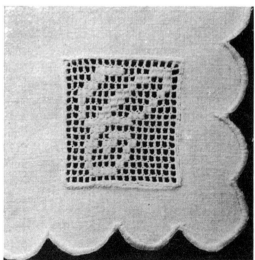

AN INITIALLED CORNER.

the last picot on a petal with the first on the next..

Finish the motif with a row of 5 d c into each sp all round. Tack the motif in place on the corner; then top-sew it neatly to the linen through the edge of the d c. Remove the tacking thread and cut away the linen from the back of the motif, leaving just enough of an edge to work buttonhole stitch over at each side.

### A Simple Motif in Cut-Work.

The illustration showing a corner with a simple motif in " cut-work " has a Venetian crochet border. This serviette is worked in colour.

For the edging you draw a thread from the linen about an eighth of an inch from the edge, all round. Through the tiny sp left in the linen by this line, you insert the crochet-hook and work d c closely all round, using fine mercerised cotton, in any colour to match the china tea service, or in white if preferred.

*2nd Row.*—Put 9 ch 1 d c into every 6th d c on the edge.

*3rd Row.*—11 d c into each loop.

*4th Row.*—9 ch 1 d c into the centre d c (6th) on each loop of last row.

*5th Row.*—* 11 d c into first loop, 6 d c into next loop, 9 ch, turn these back and fasten with a d c to the 6th d c on first loop, turn and into this top loop put 6 d c 6 ch 6 d c, 5 d c into next loop, then repeat from *.

Any simple design can be drawn or transferred to the corner ; the edges are worked over in buttonhole stitch and bars of a single thread are stitched from side to side occasionally to keep the motif in place. This thread is worked over in the button-hole stitch when recrossing, and all

this is done before the linen is cut away from the back of the design.

### An Initialled Corner.

This design shows a scalloped border in buttonhole stitch over a thick padding. These scallops are easily drawn on the edge of the linen by the aid of coins. A shilling and a florin were used alternately in this design ; place the coins along the edge, about an eighth of an inch from the outside, and mark the outer half with a pencil on the linen, then move the coin back so that the edge of it is about three-sixteenths of an inch from the pencil line ; now mark the edge of the coin on the linen again and you have the double lines for the buttonholing.

Pad between the two rows of out-lining, run through the pencilled lines, and work buttonhole stitch over with medium fine embroidery cotton.

In this serviette we show the new corner inset in filet crochet work, where the groundwork is of crochet filet squares, and the initial is worked in darning-stitch with embroidery cotton.

For the latter purpose the initial or monogram can be done in colour, or silk thread if liked.

For the filet groundwork allow 3 ch s for each square required, and 5 ch for the turning. Each mesh consists of 2 ch s, with a tr at each side.

When the square is finished with a row of d c worked closely around it, and the initial darned into it, it is ready to be sewn in place on the corner ; then the linen is cut away from the back, and the edges of the linen worked over in buttonhole stitch.

# About Ancient Cut=Work.

White embroidery is having a great vogue. This is true, not alone of the eyelet embroidery of everyday use, but the more elaborate style, known as ancient cut embroidery or art embroidery, is coming into more frequent use. Specimens of this splendid work are to be found in the

1. EMBROIDERED MONOGRAM WITH OPEN LETTERS.

museums of the principal cities of Europe, especially at museums in Italy and the Musée de Cluny, in France, where rare and priceless specimens of very ancient needlecraft are treasured. On some of these, nimble fingers have represented scenes of everyday life of the olden times—a party of hunters, the arrival of pilgrims at a castle, a tournament, etc.; on other pieces are cleverly disposed coats-of-arms or other heraldic emblems. All the details are very clearly defined, and all done by the means of the cut-out outlines or odd-shaped open spaces and eyelets filled with fine bars.

This beautiful work has been modernised to adapt it to our requirements, but still retains its originality and distinctive character, and lends itself readily to simpler compositions for adorning and decorating the home, and almost every linen display con-

tains table or household linen thus decorated. The name, Ancient Embroidery, is applied rather to the particular style of the design, to the general effect obtained, than to the execution of the work itself. But in the modern as well as the ancient pieces, insertions of embroidered filet or of Cluny are used, adding to the beauty of the work. In olden times linen thread was used exclusively for this work, but modern needlewomen prefer cotton, as it is more easily worked than linen thread. This embroidery alone is exceedingly striking, but with the addition of squares, bands or insertions of embroidered filet, Cluny or Guipure de Venise, it will produce rich and decorative effects for curtains, table linen, pillows or pincushion tops, lamp-shades, and also for dress trimmings and accessories.

The work is very interesting and easy to execute. The cross-bars and outlines may be overcast, making them round or buttonholed. The buttonhole method is a distinctive style of the work, and is known as Richelieu embroidery. The overcast edges and bars in eyelet style, however, must be given the preference if

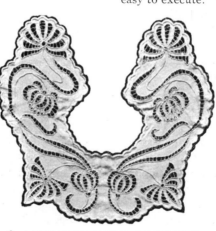

2. A GOOD EXAMPLE OF ROMAN CUT-WORK.

one desires to obtain the real ancient Roman embroidery effect, as the eyelet embroidery only will give the exact effect and style so much admired in antique specimens of the work. The buttonhole or Richelieu stitch was seldom if ever used in the olden times, and its use gives the work

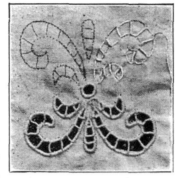

5. WORKING THE BARS AND RUNNING THE OUTLINE.

a more modern appearance. The execution is very simple, its chief quality consisting in the symmetry of the stitches; this point is essential. Linen of rather heavy quality is used for most of this work, but for squares and inserts for curtains finer fabric is sometimes used. The working thread should correspond.

After the outline has been traced on the linen, as for any other kind of

7. EMBROIDERED MONOGRAM WITH SOLID LETTERS.

white embroidery, the part to be worked on is tightly stretched on heavy stiff paper; then all the cross-bars are worked. In illustration III. are working details of three kinds of cross-bars. For the first the rounded cross-bar threads are stretched from one side of the outline to the opposite side, and the bar is made by twisting the working-thread closely and evenly around these first threads, working

tightly, so as to obtain a well-rounded bar. The third detail shows the working of the buttonholed bar, which must also be closely and evenly worked to obtain a good result. This bar must be flat. The detail at the centre shows a bar seldom used now, but frequently seen in specimens of

4. DETAIL OF RICHELIEU WORK, THE BARS AND OUTLINE BUTTONHOLED.

old embroidery. This bar, known as the flat bar, is worked on two threads stretched, as directed, from one side of the outline to the other. The working thread is then passed alternately over and under each thread, care being taken to have the stitches placed very close to each other and worked very evenly.

When all the bars are executed one

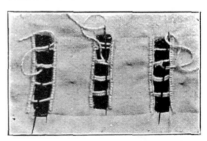

3. DETAILS OF OVERCAST, WOVEN AND BUTTONHOLED BARS.

proceeds to work on the outline. At illustrations IV. and V. is shown the method of outlining the edge of the opening and laying the foundation threads for the bars. By most workers these two parts of the work are conducted in one operation, though different workers of skill have different methods, which they have worked out to their own satisfaction. There can be no objection to this, as long as results are equally good. The outline of the design must be run with a thread, just as all eyelet edges must be prepared. The method usually employed, and here illustrated, is to make one or two small running stitches on one side of the outline, then carry the thread across the opposite side and make a corresponding number of stitches in the outline there, then back again to the starting side. Continue around the figure in this manner, making the cross-over threads at equal distances apart.

When all are laid, begin to work back, crossing from one side to the other in the same manner, but this time closely overcasting the foundation cross-threads and making the running stitches in the outline spaces, where they were omitted the first

time around. If heavier bars are desired more than one thread may be laid at each crossing, catching each with a small stitch into the outline. If two threads are laid the working back on them will bring the thread again to the same position as if only one were laid across. In heavier working, if three threads are desired for the bar foundations, the overcasting on them will bring the thread back again to the starting side.

All the outlining must be evenly done to ensure an edge of uniform size. Additional outlining, other than that run when the bars are made, is often desirable, in order to give to the outlines the rounded or corded effect which is distinctive of this work.

The linen is cut away under the bars when the work is entirely finished ; in other parts, where there are eyelets or small open spaces without bars, the linen is cut away, as in working eyelet embroidery.

The collar design is a style used extensively for the large stiff collars of the Médicis period. The execution of this pattern does not require much time, as, in order to obtain the characteristic effect, it must be worked with a comparatively coarse thread, and a very coarse thread is used for the foundation thread or filling, so as to provide for a very rounded outline, giving a decided relief. The

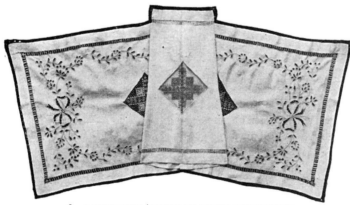

6. A SIDEBOARD RUNNER IN ROMAN EMBROIDERY
WITH INSET LACE SQUARES.

outside edges are buttonholed with coarse embroidery cotton.

A design of long floral sprays tied by a wide bow is disposed at each end of the sideboard runner. Three squares of antique filet lace are evenly placed in the plain linen centre of the runner. Embroidery and filet is often seen in the rarest and most beautiful specimens of old embroidery.

The letters are worked in the same manner as the other articles here described, only a finer thread or cotton must be selected for the embroidery, as well as for the foundation, when these letters are used for the decoration of handkerchiefs or on very thin fabrics. The chief quality in this case is the neatness of the outlines in order to bring out the shape of the letter as much as possible without giving a too heavy appearance to the work.

In the first monogram the letters are open spaces edged with overhanding and crossed by overhanded bars. In the second (illustration VII.), on the contrary, the letter is solid, of the fabric, with an open background filled with bars and wheels.

There is another variation of this form of work, to which is given the name Venetian embroidery. Its distinguishing characteristic is a heavily under-padded buttonholed edge. Though the overcast edge of the old Roman embroidery was run and padded at will to give a heavily rounded effect, the buttonholed edges of the Richelieu work were flat—this being distinctive of that more modern class of work. The Venetian combines the two characteristics into one variety. The buttonholed edge is under-padded, the skein of padding threads being couched down to the outline by short stitches, crossing it at right angles and at short intervals. This kind of padding is possible because the linen is not cut away until after the buttonholed edges are worked. While this is not unusual in buttonholing, it is a detail that makes the Roman embroidery differ completely from the English or Madeira eyelet open-work, to which at first glance it seems kin.

The designs for this work are necessarily so broad in form that almost any needle-worker may make her own or adapt them from lace designs. Large figures may be given greater variety by work on the solid petals, that may give a certain effect of shading.

This Baby's frock was designed and made by an old lady of 88. Her idea

was to show that fragments of material never need be wasted.

# Piece Rugs for Cottage Floors.

For the stone floors of country cottages, or for any floor where hard wear is the order of the day, and a good thickness under foot is acceptable, there is nothing to equal the old-fashioned Piece Rugs. They last a lifetime, and to the housewife who is "thorough" in her ways, they have the additional advantage of washing well. The following rugs I have seen in use, and can guarantee that they will wear.
—Editor.

## The Piece Rug made from Clippings.

The type best known in England is the Cloth Piece Rug. For this, pieces of cloth about 3 inches long by ¾ inch wide are required. They may be stitched on to a piece of canvas the required size; but I have found that a knitted piece rug is easier to do and wears better.

Use Strutt's No. 4 Unbleached Knitting Cotton (green tie), and a pair of thick steel needles. As this work is heavy, the rug is knit in strips, which are afterwards sewn together. Therefore cast on whatever seems a convenient number of stitches for the length of the needles, only they should be divisible by four.

Knit 6 rows plain. Then knit 3, and taking a "piece" in your hand, place it between the needles so that half the piece comes out at the front of the work, (i.e., the side nearest to you) while the other half projects at the back of the work, as shown

in the first illustration; the portion at the back of the work should be slightly longer than the portion in front. Then knit a stitch, drawing the cotton very tightly, so that the piece of cloth is gripped firmly somewhere about halfway along its length.

Now take the piece at the back, and bring it forward between the two needles, so that both the ends now show on the front of the work. Pull this well through, so as to avoid leaving any slack loop at the back, and then fix it in place by knitting the next stitch as tightly as possible. See the second illustration. It is most important that the cotton should be held as firmly as possible, otherwise, if the knitting is loose, the pieces will not be held securely and will drop out whenever the rug is shaken. Knit 3 stitches between each "piece" in the row, and end the row with three or four stitches, to allow enough for sewing together. Every "piece row" is done in this way, and 6 plain rows

The specimen at the top shows the first stage of the clipping after it has been placed in the work and a stitch knit. The lower specimen shows the second stage, after the back half has been brought through to the front and the knitting continued.

should be knit between the "piece rows."

This is really all there is in the making of these rugs, though, of course, much ingenuity can be displayed in the way of designs, only in that case much depends on the materials at your disposal. A border of one colour is always advisable, and as people usually have more black pieces than any other colour, one often sees these rugs with a black border two or three inches wide all round. If you have any quantity of red clippings, a red Greek cross or a star can be made in the centre of the rug. To do anything in the way of a pattern, you must make up your mind how large your rug is to be and count up exactly the number of rows that will be required to bring you to the place where the star or cross is to be, and then work out your design just as you would do a pattern in cross-stitch — only you knit in a coloured clipping instead of working a coloured cross-stitch.

If you decide to have an ornamental design in the middle, it is simplest to knit the centre strip first, which will include this design, then add the other strips to it. But in any case, quite a presentable rug can be made in what is called "hit and miss" pattern, i.e., just by using whatever piece comes next, irrespective of colour; and unless you have a large number of clippings in any one colour, to allow you ample for a design, the haphazard way is the safest, because it is tiresome, when you have a design nearly finished, to discover that all your clippings of that colour are exhausted.

A backing of stout canvas gives strength to the rug, though it is not imperative.

A word is necessary as to the kind of material to use. For a knitted piece rug, the clippings must all be woollen; even then any sort of woollen material will not do. A firm cloth, not too thick, is the best. If it is too thick, it is difficult to knit in properly; if it is not firmly woven, it ravels out and is very unsatisfactory for wear. Serge is useless for this work, and so are all similar materials that fray at the edge when cut. Closely-woven tweeds are all right, but not the looser weaves that ravel directly. Sometimes you can buy bundles of patterns and odd pieces from a tailor, and where much of the dressmaking is done at home there is certain to be plenty of oddments in the Piece drawer. Discarded cloth coats or skirts when washed can be cut up into a fine selection of clippings; indeed, you will be surprised to find what a pile of waste scraps there are in most households that could be turned to account in this way.

I would warn you that you should wear a pinafore or overall when knitting these rugs, as the bits from the clippings and threads always get on to one's dress at first.

## New England Rag-Mats.

When travelling in the United States of America, one comes upon all sorts of ingenuities in the way of homely rugs; in New England and many out-of-the-way villages in other States, circular braided rugs are seen on the floors in cottages and farms. These are made in a variety of ways, though the main principle is the same; old stuff is knitted or crocheted into something approaching a rope, and this is then coiled round and round (starting from the centre) till a round or oval mat is formed of the

## Piece Rugs.

desired size. In most of these rugs cotton materials can be used. Here is one method. Tear up any done-with sheets, curtains, pieces of print, flannelette, and suchlike cotton materials—washed first, of course—into strips about an inch wide. Sew each length on to the next, and wind into big balls, just as you would wind cotton. When you have accumulated about 20 pounds of this, start to

DETAILS ARE SHOWN HERE OF THE MAT DESIGNED TO WEAR WELL.

crochet with a huge wooden crochet-hook (often cut by the New England father or brother from a hickory stick). Make 12 or 20 ch, enough to join in a ring, then work as many d c into this as it will conveniently hold, and another row around outside this, and so on, row after row, increasing every row, of course, till you have a mat the size required.

Sometimes the strips are plaited and then joined together, like straw plaiting on a hat.

Another very serviceable rug I saw was made with some strips of cotton material, as described above, and cord similar to clothes-line or box-cord. For this, the rag-strip was again used just as you would do crochet cotton, and d c was worked all along over the cord, precisely as you would work d c over a padding cord in Irish crochet. As this proceeded, it was coiled round and round and sewn in place with stout thread. It makes a very thick mat underfoot.

A third rug I saw was simply strips of rags knit up into a rug on two very thick wooden needles; though I do not think this looks as well as the crochet varieties. Moreover, it is rather flimsy.

I have made a mat myself which combines several of the characteristics of these rag mats. It may not be a novelty, but, at any rate, I have never seen one like it. The object of this is to enable all sorts of materials to be used up, and yet for the mat to have a wool finish. It is also firmer than some of the rag mats.

Join together into strips any sort of waste material you may have by you, so long as it is all about the same degree of thickness and pliability— ribbons, cottons, flannel, cashmere, delaine—any oddments, in fact, that will allow themselves to be joined together into strips. Then take three lengths of this, tie them very tightly together at the top, and plait them as firmly as you can. If you get to the end of a strip, join on another ; go on plaiting till you have a good hank done. Tie the end of this very tightly again, to prevent it unplaiting.

Now you will want all the odd balls and skeins of wool you can lay hands on—the thicker the better. With a stout bone hook work d c over the plait to cover it completely with the wool. The doubles want to be as close together as possible, so as to allow the upper edge to " give," when the rope is curved, without gaping and showing the cotton plait beneath. This can either be coiled round after a length is completed, and sewn together at the back with wool or thread, or it can be caught together with the crochet - hook every few stitches as you go along.

The illustration shows you a section of the " plait " at the right-hand side —this identical plait was composed of a strand of old cotton sheeting torn into strips, a strand of old ribbons, and the list edge from flannel. A mixture of material is an advantage. The rest of this diagram shows the wool being added in d c (use any colours just as they come) and the rope being coiled.

The mat is rather warmer than the crochet rag-mat I first described, and it has more soft "spring" in it than the mat made with the cord. Moreover, it does not absorb the damp as much as the all-cotton mats do.

All these rag-mats should be finished off with a piece of stout canvas at the back.

Also it should be noted that the mats will wash.

A Centre-piece of Cream Congress Canvas with a cross-stitch
design of purple grapes and green leaves.

# Combining Canvas & Crochet.

One of the beauties of crochet lace is its adaptability. Among the most desirable kinds are those made up of separate motifs that suggest numerous possibilities, involving only slight changes.

Borders for centrepieces or table-covers of linen, scrim, canvas and similar fabrics have the foundation crocheted directly into the material. In all loosely-woven fabrics the crochet

A CENTREPIECE OF JAVA CANVAS WORKED IN CROSS-STITCH AND WITH CROCHETED BORDER.

hook (it is invariably steel for this kind of work) penetrates the cloth readily. If there is any difficulty a large pin or needle may be used to make the holes. Keep them at even spaces, and be careful that the ch stitches between the trs correspond in length with these sp.

There are two or three points that are important in making good crochet, and this is one of them;

A TABLE-COVER OF CONGRESS CANVAS WITH CROCHET EDGE OF ECRU COTTON.

the size of the hook and the method of working are others. Generally speaking, the crochet-hook should be as fine as will work the thread readily, and the stitches should be moderately tight. There is no firmness and precision to the work that is done very loosely. A row of d c or tr should always be started with a ch whose length shall equal the height of the stitches in the row. The round is then completed (if the work progresses in rounds) by slip-stitching, after the last stitch, into the last stitch of the ch at the beginning.

The centre-piece illustrated is made of ivory canvas, divided into blocks by 3 rows of threads run straight across the material in over-and-under darnings. Each block measures 22 threads each way. The cross-

DETAIL OF CROCHET ON CENTREPIECE.

stitch design may readily be followed from the illustration, reckoning 2 threads of the canvas for every cross-stitch or space. Coloured Ososilkie is suitable for the cross-stitch, and Ardern's White Crochet Cotton No. 36 for the crochet edge, which is begun with 4 rows of insertion worked around the entire centrepiece.

### The Insertion.

One row of 2 ch, 1 tr, 2 ch, 1 tr is worked around entire cover, with an extra stitch in each corner.

2nd Row.—5 ch, 1 s c between every two tr of the first row.

3rd Row.—5 ch, 1 s c around 5 ch in former row, * 5 ch, 4 tr around

next 5 ch in former row, 5 ch, 1 s c. Repeat from * around the four sides of the cover, putting 8 tr with 5 ch between in each corner.

4th Row.—5 ch, * 1 s c at the beginning of 4 tr, 5 ch, 1 s c at end of 4 tr, 5 ch, and repeat from *.

### The Wheel.

Wrap your cotton around a good-sized lead-pencil ten or twelve times, slip off, and on this ring work 3 ch and 23 tr : slip-stitch last stitch to third ch at beginning of row.

2nd Row.—3 ch, 1 s c into every stitch of former row.

3rd Row.—3 ch, 1 tr, in the same stitch, 5 ch, 2 tr into every other loop of 3 ch of former row, slip-stitch last 5 ch to third ch at beginning of row.

4th Row.—1 s c into first tr in former row, 4 ch, 1 tr into third ch on former row ; 5 ch, * slip-stitch into first ch, 5 ch, slip-stitch into same stitch, 5 ch, slip-stitch into same stitch. (This makes a cluster of 3 picots of 5 ch each.) 4 ch, 1 s c into second tr, 4 ch, 1 tr into third ch on former row, 5 ch, and repeat from *.

The wheels are joined together in the making, and to the insertion with

## Combining Canvas and Crochet.

the last row, by making 2 ch of the centre loop in picot and catching to the next wheel with a slip-stitch ; 2 ch, and finishing as above.

### The Cross between the Wheels.

Work to the centre picot—making 2 of the 5 ch, then 4 ch, 1 tr in the third ch ; now holding the wheel towards you, work 3 tr around the loop of 5 ch on the insertion, 3 tr around next loop of 5 ch and slip off all stitches at once ; 3 ch to top of picot, 2 ch to finish picot, and continue as before and finish wheel.

When joining next wheel, work the other 3 tr to finish the cross into same centre stitch, and continue as shown in illustration.

### The Table=Cover.

The insertion around the scrim or Congress canvas cover is the same as that around the centre-piece described, but there are two rows of the clusters of 4 tr. This would look well in *écru* crochet cotton.

The lace is worked back and forth and joined to the insertion with a single crochet at the end of every other row.

Make a ch of 40 stitches, turn, and into the fourth ch and next 2 ch work 1 tr ; 2 ch, 1 tr into every third ch 6 times ; 2 ch, 1 tr into each of next 13 ch ; 9 ch, turn.

*2nd Row.*—1 tr into first 3 ch and into every tr in former row and 3 tr over ch in former row (19 tr) ; 2 ch, 1 tr, five times ; 2 ch, 4 tr to end. Catch to insertion with 1 s c, 3 ch, turn.

*3rd Row.*—3 tr, 2 ch, 1 tr five times ; 9 tr, 2 ch, 1 s c into third tr of former

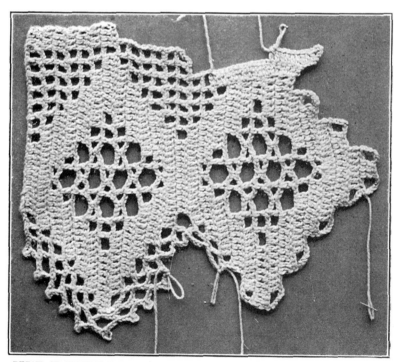

DETAIL OF CROCHET FOR SCRIM COVER.

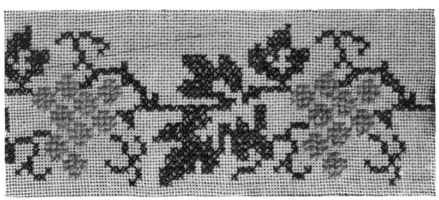

A WORKING DETAIL OF THE
CROSS-STITCH DESIGN ON PAGE 55.

*Peri-Lusta shade No. 419 is a rich
violet. No. 414 a good green.*

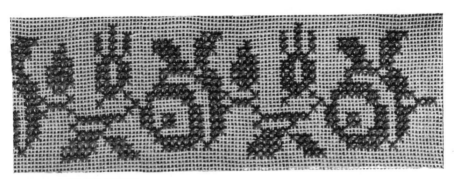

A WORKING DETAIL OF THE
CROSS-STITCH DESIGN ON PAGE 62.

row, 2 ch, 1 tr into next third tr and finish with 9 tr, 9 ch and turn.

*4th Row.*—1 tr into first 3 ch and next 7 tr; 2 ch, 1 tr; 5 ch, 1 tr; 2 ch, 10 tr; 2 ch, 1 tr 4 times, and finish as in other rows. Catch to insertion, ch 3 and turn.

*5th Row.*—3 tr, 2 ch, 1 tr, 2 ch, 1 tr, 2 ch, 10 tr, 5 ch, 1 tr, 2 ch, 1 s c into middle of 5 ch in former row, 2 ch, 1 tr, 5 ch and 10 tr to end of row, 9 ch, turn.

*6th Row.*—10 tr, 2 ch, 1 tr, 2 ch, 1 s c into middle of 5 ch, 2 ch, 1 tr, 5 ch, 2 ch, 1 s c into middle of 5 ch, 2 ch, 1 tr, 2 ch, 10 tr, and finish as in other rows—join to insertion, ch 3, and turn.

*7th Row.*—3 tr, 2 ch, 10 tr, 2 ch, 1 tr, 2 ch, 1 tr, 5 ch, 1 tr, 2 ch, 1 s c, 2 ch, 1 tr, 5 ch, 1 tr, 2 ch, 1 tr, 2 ch, 10 tr to point.

These seven rows form the half of each point, and the rows are then repeated, but with 6 ch instead of 9 at end of each.

That is, the eighth row is like sixth, ninth row like fifth, and so on. The illustration will show how the corner is fitted in.

The edge is made with one row of 5 ch, with 2 tr to fill up the corners, another row of loops of 5 ch each, and a finish of 2 ch, 1 tr, 2 ch.

59

# The Waved Line Knitting Pattern.

In order to condense the matter as much as possible, the following symbols are employed:

**S** = Slip a stitch on the next needle without knitting it.

**K** = Knit a plain stitch.

**P** = Purl.

**O** = Over; that is, put the thread forward and over the needle in order to make an extra stitch.

**N** = Narrow; that is, knit two stitches together.

WAVED LINE INSERTION.

### Insertion.

Cast on 28 stitches.

*1st Row.*—S, K, O, N, K, O, N, K 3, O, N, O, N, K 3, over and narrow 5 times, K.

*2nd Row.*—S, K, O, N, K 7, P 3, K 4, P 3, K 4, O, N, K.

*3rd Row.*—S, K, over and narrow 3 times, K 3, O, N, O, N, K 3, over and and narrow 3 times, K, O, N, K.

*4th Row.*—S, K, O, N, K 6, P 3, K 4, P 3, K 5, O, N, K.

*5th Row.*—S, K, O, N, K, O, N, O, N, K 3, O, N, O, N, K 3, over and narrow 4 times, K.

*6th Row.*—S, K, O, N, K 5, P 3, K 4, P 3, K 6, O, N, K.

*7th Row.*—S, K, over and narrow 4 times, K 3, O, N, O, N, K 3, O, N, O, N, K, O, N, K.

*8th Row.*—S, K, O, N, K 4, P 3, K 4, P 3, K 7, O, N, K.

*9th Row.*—S, K, O, N, K, over and narrow 3 times, K 3, O, N, O, N, K 3, over and narrow 3 times, K.

*10th Row.*—S, K, O, N, K 3, P 3, K 4, P 3, K 8, O, N, K.

*11th Row.*—S, K, over and narrow 5 times, K 3, O, N, O, N, K 3, O, N, K, O, N, K.

*12th Row.*—S, K, O, N, K 2, P 3, K 4, P 3, K 9, O, N, K.

*13th Row.*—S, K, O, N, K, over and narrow 4 times, K 3, O, N, O, N, K 3, O, N, O, N, K.

WAVED LINE EDGING.

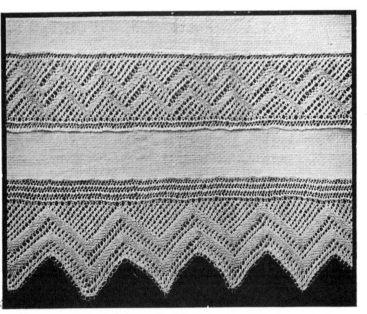

THIS SHOWS THE INSERTION AND EDGING
APPLIED TO A LINEN TOWEL.

extra stitch before knitting the first stitch), K 5, P 3, K 4, P 3, K 4, over and narrow 3 times, K.

*3rd Row.*—S, K, over and narrow 5 times, K 3, O, N, O, N, K 3, O, N, O, N, K.

*4th Row.*—O, K 5, P 3, K 4, P 3, K 5, over and narrow 3 times, K.

*5th Row.*—S, K, over and narrow 3 times, K, O, N, O, N, K 3, O, N, O, N, K 3, O, N, O, N, K.

*6th Row.*—O, K 5, P 3, K 4, P 3, K 6, over and narrow 3 times, K.

*7th Row.*—S, K, over and narrow 6 times, K 3, O, N, O, N, K 3, O, N, O, N, K.

*8th Row.*—O, K 5, P 3, K 4, P 3, K 7, over and narrow 3 times, K.

*9th Row.*—S, K, over and narrow 3 times, K, over and narrow 3 times, K 3, O, N, O, N, K 3, O, N, O, N, K.

*10th Row.*—O, K 5, P 3, K 4, P 3, K 8, over and narrow 3 times, K.

*11th Row.*—S, K, over and narrow 7 times, K 3, O, N, O, N, K 3, O, N, O, N, K.

*12th Row.*—O, K 5, P 3, K 4, P 3, K 9, over and narrow 3 times, K.

*13th Row.*—S, K, over and narrow 3 times, K, over and narrow 4 times, K 3, O, N, O, N, K 3, O, N, O, N, K.

*14th Row.*—O, K 5, P 3, K 4, P 3, K 10, over and narrow 3 times, K.

*14th Row.*—S, K, O, N, K, P 3, K 4, P 3, K 10, O, N, K.

*15th Row.*—S, K, over and narrow 5 times, K 3, O, N, O, N, K 3, O, N, K, O, N, K.

*16th Row.*—The same as the 12th row.

*17th Row.*—As the 9th Row.

*18th Row.*—As the 10th Row.

*19th Row.*—As the 7th Row.

*20th Row.*—As the 8th Row.

*21st Row.*—As the 5th Row.

*22nd Row.*—As the 6th Row.

*23rd Row.*—As the 3rd Row.

*24th Row.*—As the 4th Row.

*25th Row.*—As the 1st Row.

*26th Row.*—As the 2nd Row.

Then commence again at 1st Row.

**Edging.**

Cast on 26 stitches.

*1st Row.*—S, K, over and narrow 3 times, K, O, N, K 3, O, N, O, N, K 3, O, N, O, N, K.

*2nd Row.*—O (that is, put the thread round the needle so as to make an

## The Waved Line
## Knitting Pattern.

15*th Row* —S, K, over and narrow 8 times, K 3, O, N, O, N, K 3, O, N, O, N, K.

16*th Row.*—O, K 5, P 3, K 4, P 3, K 11, over and narrow 3 times, K.

17*th Row.*—S, K, over and narrow 3 times, K, over and narrow 4 times, K 3, O, N, O, N, K 3, O, N, O, N, K, N.

18*th Row.*—O, N, K 4, P 3, K 4, P 3, K 10, over and narrow 3 times, K.

19*th Row.* – S, K, over and narrow 7 times, K 3, O, N, O, N, K 3, O, N, O, N, K, N.

20*th Row.*—O, N, K 4, P 3, K 4, P 3, K 9, over and narrow 3 times, K.

21*st Row.*—S, K, over and narrow 3 times, K, over and narrow 3 times, K 3, O, N, O, N, K 3, O, N, O, N, K, N.

22*nd Row.*—O, N, K 4, P 3, K 4, P 3, K 8, over and narrow 3 times, K.

23*rd Row.*—S, K, over and narrow 6 times, K 3, O, N, O, N, K 3, O, N, O, N, K, N.

24*th Row.*—O, N, K 4, P 3, K 4, P 3, K 7, over and narrow 3 times, K.

25*th Row.*—S, K, over and narrow 3 times, K, over and narrow 3 times, K 3, O, N, O, N, K, N.

26*th Row.*—O, N, K 4, P 3, K 4, P 3, K 6, over and narrow 3 times, K.

27*th Row.*—S, K, over and narrow 5 times, K 3, O, N, O, N, K 3, O, N, O, N, K, N.

28*th Row.*—O, N, K 4, P 3, K 4, P 3, K 5, over and narrow 3 times, K.

29*th Row.*—S, K, over and narrow 3 times, K, O, N, K 3, O, N, O, N, K 3, O, N, O, N, K, N.

30*th Row.*—O, N, K 4, P 3, K 4, P 3, K 4, over and narrow 3 times, K.

31*st Row.*—S, K, over and narrow 4 times, K 3, O, N, O, N, K 3, O, N, O, N, K, N.

32*nd Row.*—O, N, K 4, P 3, K 4, P 3, K 3, over and narrow 3 times, K.

Repeat from 1st row.

If this insertion and edging is knit in Ardern's Crochet Cotton No. 22, it will do for huckaback towels, as illustrated on page 61. If No. 100 Ardern's Crochet Cotton is used, it will make a fine lace suitable for tray-cloths, and even for underwear. In each case the steel knitting needles must be of a size to suit the cotton.

This will also make an admirable insertion and edging for écru linen blinds, if moderately coarse steel needles are used with Ardern's Crochet Cotton No. 16, Shade 2, Medium Ivory. This cotton is a very good shade to use for curtains or blinds.

A
Cross-stitch
Border for a
Table-cloth

With
Pink Roses
and Bud and
Green leaves.

# Trimmings of
# Filet=Net and Silk Braid.

5. A BOLERO OR BRASSIÈRE, WORKED WITH BLACK BRAID
AND SILK ON BLACK NET.

13. A SOLID MOTIF.

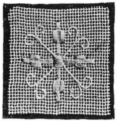

14. A LACY MOTIF

Most of the present-day filet net trimmings are worked on machine-made netting, which is far less expensive than the hand-made variety, and really preferable, as it has a very smooth and even surface. The net is obtainable in black, white and écru, and most of the leading drapers have various other colours, at a very reasonable price. For the variety of embroidery described, a very narrow flat silk braid is used, and in some cases the figures of the pattern are outlined with crochet or embroidery stitch. The braid is worked in darning stitch, passed under and over the bars of the squares as in illustration 1.

1. DARNING STITCH.

In the small figures, the braid is passed over three or four squares, according to the pattern, in a manner resembling the flat or satin stitch. The stitches must always be made with an upward motion, as this gives a better appearance to the work. To begin a new

2. A FIGURE IN
DARNING STITCH.

stitch, bring the needle down to a lower row. A tapestry needle with a dull round point is used. In large figures the braid is worked in darning stitches, passing the braid over and under every alternate bar, as in illustration 2.

To obtain a neat effect it is preferable to bring the braid back, leaving it loose, on the wrong side of the work, working the upper or right side always in the same direction. This has also the advantage of providing a sort of padding which gives to the finished work a raised effect which

## Filet Net and Silk Braid.

3. A SIMPLE BAND TRIMMING.

6. A SERPENTINE MOTIF.

makes it very attractive. The pattern should be drawn on heavy paper and the net basted over this paper. The simpler designs may be worked by counting the bars in the same manner as for cross-stitch work. It is essential to avoid twisting the narrow braid, which must always lie perfectly flat on the under side as well as on the right side; the beauty and neatness of the work depend upon this rule. When the work is done by counting the bars and squares, it is very convenient to stretch it over a small frame or hoop. Press the braid lightly between the thumb and the forefinger, to mark the crease at each end of the stitch. When the work is entirely finished, press it lightly on the wrong side with a moderately hot iron.

Illustration 3 is a simple pattern, very pretty for a blouse trimming. Cut a strip of net of the required length, and for the width count 22 squares. Two squares at each side must be turned under and run with the braid to form the border. Run the braid through the squares in darning fashion, catching into al-

4. AN EFFECTIVE BANDING EASILY MADE.

ternate squares when making the second row of braid. It is better not to cut the braid before reaching the full length of the band; the only difficulty in that case is to keep the braid from twisting, but after a little practice this is easily managed. To make the small figure, begin at the centre square, work over 2 squares with a flat stitch, working 2 stitches for each of the 4 petals. Catch the braid on the wrong side with a few stitches.

The band in illustration 4 is worked

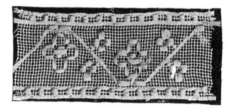

8. SERPENTINE DESIGN AND CORRESPONDING BORDER.

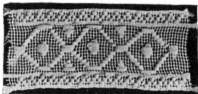

9. ANOTHER VARIETY OF THE SERPENTINE MOTIF.

with horizontal stitches only, and is very simple. A careful study of the pattern will enable anyone to succeed in making it. It is always better in this kind of work to make the stitches from left to right. Begin the squares at each side with the centre stitch, then execute the upper stitches, and last the lower stitches, bringing the needle back finally to the centre stitch of the opposite square.

The pattern in illustration 6

differs somewhat from the others in the serpentine band which runs through the centre. This band is worked in darning stitch and with four rows of braid. A small figure fills the space left at each side of the middle band. One row of squares is left between the border at the side edges and the

7. EASILY WORKED DESIGN WITH BARRED BORDER.

10. A HANDSOME DESIGN WITH BRAID AND SILK.

pattern at the centre; if, however, a wider trimming band is desired, a larger space may be allowed between the edges and the pattern. The outside border may also serve to widen the band, by selecting any of the fancy borders of the other figures. The detached figures, filling the triangles, consist of horizontal stitches. It is easy to follow this pattern by studying carefully the illustration and counting the stitches; the undulated centre band is executed first, but always after the edges are run.

The side borders of the band in illustration 7 are rather more elaborate and lend a pretty effect, especially when the trimming is to be applied to soft light material. To make this border, run first the

11. A WIDE BAND ON BLACK NET.

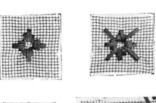

12. SOME SMALL FIGURES AND SUGGESTIONS.

outside row of straight braid and make the small bars by making 2 stitches, one below the other each over 1 square. Make the next bar by working 2 stitches into the next 2 squares. The cross-bar threads of net between will show and provide the apparent space. Make another straight row of braid to match the outside row. Begin the centre pattern at the middle of the netting, working first the right side and then the left side of the lozenge as shown in the illustration.

The band in illustration 8 is somewhat similar to illustration 6, but instead of straight bars, the stitches in the border are overhanded, one row lower at each time. A straight row of braid outlines the inner edge of each border. The pattern is formed of wide lozenges with a dot in the centre band; small dots of triangles are disposed in each point formed by the pattern near the outside border. The serpentine pattern is worked in overhand stitches, each over 3 bars of the net, and each 1 row lower and 1 row to the side of the previous stitch.

## Filet Net and Silk Braid.

In illustration 9 the edges are worked like those in illustration 7, except that the space left between the bars is one square wider. A single row of braid in darning stitch runs through the pattern in V-shape. The spaces between the points are filled by detached figures, the smaller like those described for illustration 3, and the larger composed of alternated outside and underside flat-stitch, or point lance. The centre of this figure is filled with a small dot.

The work on the band in illustration 10 is all in darning stitch, outlined with rope or crochet silk; the stems and small leaves are worked with this same silk. This method of embroidering the net gives a rich and elaborate effect. The small figures may be made in flat-stitch, and in that case they are not outlined with silk; this combination of the two stitches gives charming variety. For the execution of the large figures follow the directions for illustration 2.

Illustration 11 shows another example of the work obtainable with braid on net. The figures in the centre are executed in flat-stitch, both vertical and horizontal; the stems and small figures are worked with crochet silk in cross-stitch; the wide border at each side consists of two straight rows of braid outlining a small pattern, worked with the silk in cross-stitch. This pattern is especially well adapted for bretelles, front bands and also for insertion or panels on skirts made of light materials.

Illustration 12 shows some of the stitches used in the bolero-blouse or brassière. The small sprays and leaves are made with crochet silk in darning stitches.

Illustrations 13 and 14 show two figures that may be used as insertions or on trimming bands similar to those illustrated here. They are made in a combination of the various stitches described.

# A Serviette Case.

A case for the serviette is a French idea that is useful as well as ornamental. It will especially appeal to ladies living in boarding-houses, or any other place where the serviette is placed with many others.

It is also useful to put in a trunk when travelling. Make just like a wide envelope with a flap coming right over the front. We give a suggestion for a design that could be embroidered on the flap.

# Resille Net.

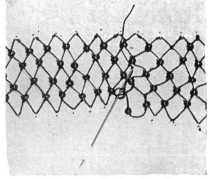

Showing how the Knot is made.

One of the fashion ideas from Paris is the new " Resille " beaded net, which is being largely used by all the best dressmakers both in Paris and London at the present moment in making up the costumes for the coming season. This net is entirely hand-made, and as the beads are all placed over the knots, it can be cut in every direction without any danger of becoming unravelled. Needless to say, this novelty is very expensive to purchase, costing from about 14s. to 20s. a yard 16 inches wide, yet it is very easily made, and if a little tedious at first, it soon becomes so fascinating in the making that one leaves it with reluctance.

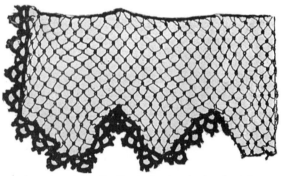

A section of a Collar Band, showing the Crochet Edge.

Resille is seen in a combination of two colours generally, and all black, or white. For evening wear, white with gold or silver beads is the most elegant.

We show a section of a collar band of black, which, with the usual stiffening, can be mounted over white satin or any of the prevailing colours. It is finished with a little edging of crochet, as is the piece of lace suitable for trimming a negligé or a bolero, making a berthe, or trimming an evening blouse.

The net is made over a mesh with a sewing needle. For the black net use thread No. 15, black, and form the first row of stitches over a supplementary thread formed into a loop, just as in the ordinary netting.

Use a one-eighth inch mesh. To form the knot, shown in Fig. 1, pass the needle under the loop below and under the thread make a loop round the needle and pull up the thread, put a bead on the thread, make another loop, keeping the bead on the back of the mesh while pulling it up, then pass the needle and thread through the bead again, upwards, put on another bead and make another loop, and treat the bead in the same way as last.

The net can be cut into any shape, and afterwards finished with the edging as shown.

The practised worker of filet net will find no difficulty in making little round motifs, and squares or diamonds, as all the fancy net stitches can be worked with this knot stitch.

# Ornamenting Flannel Garments.

This page offers some suggestions for the ornamentation of flannel garments, such as underskirts, winter night-dresses, dressing-gowns and dressing-jackets. Work of this kind is very easy to do, and moreover is quickly done; hence it well repays one for the trouble expended upon it.

For anyone who is at all nervous, and who therefore finds fine sewing or elaborate fancy-work trying, this work is to be recommended, as it lacks what may be termed the "fidgeting"

A simple idea that gives variety to the trimming of a flannel underskirt.

This spray is worked in pink wool, the darker lines being in deep rose silk.

This design would be very serviceable for the bottom of a petticoat. It is here shown in shades of red.

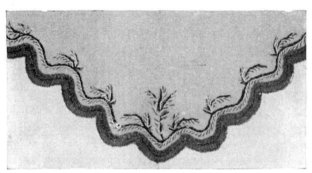

A trimming that would be useful for the collar of a dressing-jacket. The edges are button-holed in blue, and the inside feather-stitching is in blue and gold silk.

qualities of ordinary sewing. Being soft, it is easy to work upon, and the stitches are not so fine as those needed in other forms of sewing.

Another advantage of this work lies in the fact that simple sprays are often more effective than elaborate designs, and the worker who has the very slightest knowledge of embroidery, can work a design as she goes along, without having any tracing. Branching sprays, little stars, feathery scrolls are all pretty, and a buttonholed edge is always the best finish.

The design at the top of the page shows

This is a pretty design for a corner of the collar of a dressing gown, or for a flannel nightdress.

The material here used is a soft grey, and the embroidery is done in a delicate green wool.

how the bottom of a flannel skirt can be given a light effect by the introduction of a little lace or fancy-edging. The flannel is cut out in tabs, and button-holed all round, and the lace is applied at the back, so that it frills up between the tabs.

For embroidering flannel in white or cream, remember that mercerised cotton or linen thread wears much better than either silk or wool, and it looks as well as either. In many cases the coloured mercerised cottons do as well as wools for embroidering flannels. We specially recommend the Peri Lusta Esplend'or Threads, for this work — they are made for using on flannel.

This is an elaborate crochet design appliquéd to the material. It would look very handsome on a dressing-gown. This piece was worked in two shades of violet.

# Needlepoints.

Accustom yourself to wearing a finger-shield on the first finger of the left hand when doing sewing. Though it may seem awkward at first, one quickly grows used to it, and by this means the unsightly roughness will be prevented that results from the needle pricks.

It is better to use a crochet hook with the needle portion the same thickness throughout, as it produces more even work than where the needle is gradually enlarged to form the handle.

A cord made of single ch stitch with a coarse crochet hook and thick cotton is very serviceable for threading in the tops of vests, etc., instead of a ribbon. It launders well.

# Bead Embroidery on Net.

A very attractive novelty of present day fashion is bead embroidery on net. Small porcelain beads, principally in white, are elaborately embroidered on black net or other material, and this is used not only for trimming purposes, but for tunics, blouses, etc. Jet beads are also very fashionable, and silver on black ninon de soie is a favourite for half mourning. Of course, bugles and spangles can be employed for variety in combination with other beads.

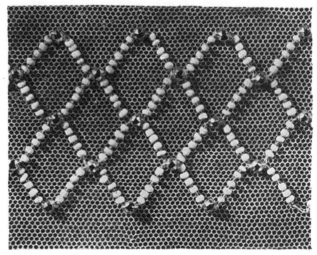
No. 1.—An All-over Design for a Blouse.

The embroidery is very easily made, and many lovely designs can be easily carried out on the net, as the lines of the meshes lend themselves to the formation of geometrical figures. Use a thread sufficiently fine to pass through the eye of a number 8 sewing needle. In making lines run the thread through the mesh, taking up a bead for each, and at the end of each line knot the thread around the strand between the last and next mesh.

No. 1 shows an all-over design for blouses, etc. There are 5 white porcelain beads at each side of the trellis, and these lines are connected by a large silver bead. The diagonal lines in the net are used as guides. A little experience will enable anyone to work this design very quickly.

No. 2 —Suitable for Bands of Trimming on Blouse or Tunic.

No. 2 is a design suitable for trimming a tunic or blouse ; and here, also, the only

No. 3.—A Good Insertion or Edging.

guide required to carry out the design are the lines in the net.

No. 3 shows a trimming suitable for neck or sleeve bands, insertion edging, or other purpose. In this design small glass bugles and beads are employed. The edges of the net are turned under at each side, and a heading of beads worked on.

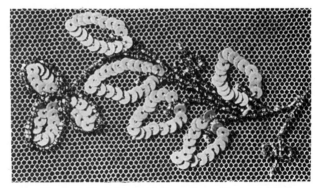

No. 4 —A Floral Design to be used as a Single Motif.

Fasten the thread to the edge, put on three beads, and fasten with a knot-stitch to the next mesh, taking care to have the 3 beads standing up in the shape of a trefoil. Whip over the edge of next 3 meshes, and repeat the 3 beads, and so on to the end. Run 2 rows of beads with a line of meshes between them immediately below the heading.

No. 4 shows a floral design suitable for employing as a single motif, or being repeated for trimming purposes. Bluish green glass beads are used for the stems and outlines, and white iridescent spangles of a small size are used for the leaves. These are sewn on in such a way that they overlap each other. For this design it will be advantageous to copy the outline on a piece of white paper, and tack the net over it, the lines can then be easily and quickly followed.

No. 5 shows a simple pattern that is easily done

A great variety of beads suitable for embroidery on net can be obtained from Mr. Rogier, 14, High Street, Kensington, W.; Mr. John Allen, 263, Oxford Street, W.; Mr. William Barnard, 126, Edgware Road, W.

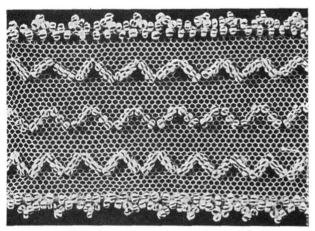

No. 5.—A Trimming that is quickly done.

Have you seen the "Home Art Crochet Book"? * It contains 148 illustrations, with full directions for working each Design. Uniform with this Volume. Price 1/- net. Postage 4d. extra.

* Available from Dover Publications, Inc. Visit our website, **www.doverpublications.com**, or write to Dover Publications, 31 East 2nd Street, Mineola, NY 11501 for availability and price.

# Samples of Drawn=Thread Work.

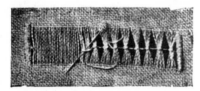

1.—THREADS TIED IN GROUPS.

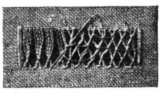

2.—THREADS CLUSTERED AT THE EDGES, THEN TIED IN GROUPS.

Drawn-thread work is one of the oldest forms of art needlework. Elaborate designs are seen in the ancient Italian models, though at that early time the loosened strands were united by threads that were drawn out from the textile. Now linen or crochet threads, matching those of the linen or a trifle finer or coarser, are used for this purpose, the drawn threads, especially when the material chosen is of a very fine texture, making it too fragile.

Drawn-work is used for decoration of table and household linen, children's dresses, ladies' blouses, sideboard cloths, cushion covers, d'oileys, and a multitude of other articles. Indeed it would be difficult to say where drawn-thread work may *not* be used !

3.—SINGLE CROSSING.

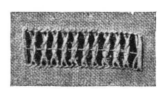

4.—SINGLE CROSSING WITH THREADS CLUSTERED AT THE EDGES.

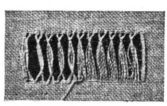

5.—CLUSTERING AND GROUPING THE THREADS.

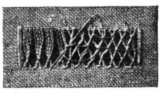

6—WORKING THE GROUPS INTO LATTICE.

The outfit is very simple, consisting only of fine, sharp, steel needles, embroidery scissors, and, if possible, an ivory thimble; when the linen is of a very fine texture, a large magnifying glass will be found necessary when drawing the threads.

When ready to work, the entire piece of linen may be stretched on a large square frame, or a small part only may be worked on at a time, and stretched over a small round or oblong embroidery hoop.

It is a better plan to measure the width of the material to be worked on than to count the number of threads, as the threads are in most cases of uneven coarseness. When the measures are carefully taken and lightly marked with a fine-pointed pencil, the threads are cut at the required limits, and then carefully drawn out. The *cut* edges should always be button-holed.

Illustration 1 shows the threads removed in one direction, leaving a band of loose strands ready to be clustered by knots. The stitch used in this case is similar to the chain stitch. Tack the working thread to the middle at the one

72

end of the band, pass the threaded needle over the working thread and under the required number of strands, bring the thread across the loose strands and pass it under the point of the needle, to form a loop, pull the knot tightly and work the next cluster in the same manner. The position of the needle is shown in illustration 1.

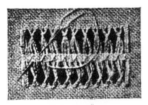

7.—CLUSTERING WITH CROSS-STITCH.

In illustration 2 is shown how the loose strands are clustered at the edges of the band and afterwards re-united in groups; both edges must be worked in the same direction, from left to right. When the threads have been clustered along both edges (care should be taken to have the clusters

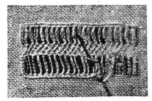

8.—SINGLE AND DOUBLE HERRINGBONE STITCH.

matching on both sides), the clusters are caught in groups of three or more; this grouping of the clusters is done by the method described above for the clustering of single threads.

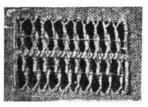

9.—A COMBINATION OF SEVERAL STITCHES.

Illustration 3 shows one of the easiest and quickest ways of working drawn threads. The single crossing is done by separating the threads into sets or clusters of four strands or more, two of these sets forming the pattern. The working thread is started at the left and in the middle of the band of loose strands. Pass the needle over two sets and bring it back, from right to left under the second and over the first, and then from left to right under

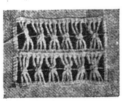

10.—A DOUBLE ROW OF CLUSTERING.

both sets, and pull the thread. Repeat the process until you reach the opposite end of the band.

Stitch No. 4 is worked like No. 3 with the exception that the edges are clustered. The clustering must be done first, then follow the directions given for No. 3.

Illustration 5 shows the beginning, and No. 6 a further development of the same stitch into a lattice design. The edges are first clustered, and the clusters caught in groups of two, the working thread being whipped up and down in the following manner: First catch three threads at the upper left edge, whip the working thread down towards the middle of the band; when about one-fourth of the way across the band, catch six threads together, then whip the thread towards the edge again and cluster the second set of three threads; when both edges are thus finished, bring the working thread to the middle of the band and divide the groups, alternating the cluster with those on the edges.

In illustration 7 the outer edges are worked as in No. 5. A narrow band is left between the two wider bands of loose strands; the threads dividing the strands at each edge of the narrow linen band form a cross-stitching over this band.

## Samples of
## Drawn-Thread Work.

The design in illustration 8 is composed of two narrow bands of loose strands divided by a narrow band of linen. At each outside edge the loose strands are clustered by single herring bone stitching. Double herringbone or coral stitch divides the strands at each side of

11.—HOW TO FILL A CORNER.

14.—FOUNDATION THREADS AND PLAIN WHEEL.

the narrow band in the middle, at the same time affording a decoration on this band.

The pattern in illustration 9 includes the stitches described at Nos. 3 and 4; the narrow band of linen left at the centre is covered by cross-stitching, worked over the band, and serving to divide the strands by clusters of three.

In illustration 10 the loose strands are clustered (three of them) at both edges by single herringbone stitching; a narrow band of linen, left in the middle, is ornamented by herringbone or coral stitching, which is used to divide the clusters at both sides. At the middle of each band of loose strands the working thread is tacked, the clusters are loosely caught by a knot, and a wheel is

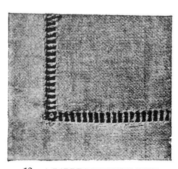

12.—A LADDER-STITCHED HEM.

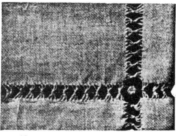

13.—HEMSTITCHING IN GROUPED CLUSTERS.

worked at the centre of each group.

Illustration 11. This design is about one and a quarter inches wide; the edges are stitched at each side, the outside edges of the square hole forming the corner are button holed and the band is worked in single-crossing like No. 3. When reaching the square space at the corner, * buttonhole the lower part of the last cluster on about three-eighths of an inch, whip the working thread at the same distance to the opposite buttonholed edge of the square, bring the thread to the corner and whip it to the opposite corner, tack it to the buttonholed edge at about three-eighths of an inch underneath and whip it to the opposite last cluster, then buttonhole this cluster on about three-eighths of an inch. Tack the thread to the upper side of this cluster, and work again from *. When the foundation threads are in position, work over each set of three threads to form a cross, tapering near the centre. Fill the centre with a wheel.

Illustration 12 shows

15 and 16.—A SPECIAL WHEEL AND AN EIGHT-POINT STAR.

a hemstitched corner, which is very simple ; the loose strands are divided at each edge by hemstitching, forming a ladder, and the small open space, left at the c o r n e r, i s worked with a wheel.

In illustration 13 the bands of loose strands are carried to the edges. The hem is first carefully basted with under and u p p e r edges perfectly even, then b o t h e d g e s a r e caught in the hemstitching, that is also used to divide the clusters o f l o o s e strands (3 strands f o r e a c h cluster). Then the band is worked as directed for No. 2. The open space is filled by a

A Handy Bag of linen, trimmed with rows of Featherstitching.

wheel. The working threads used for the bands are continued over the open space and used as foundation threads. In fine hemstitching, this space, where the two bands of loose strands meet, forming an open square, is too small to be filled, but when the open-work bands are wide the squares at the corners are correspondingly large, and they are always filled with wheels that may be simple or elaborate in correspondence with the general character of the design.

In illustration 14 the foundation threads of a wheel are shown, and also the manner of working on these threads. Practically any number of threads may be laid for the foundation,

but it must be an even number. For the ordinary wheel, from four to eight are used. They cross, diagonally, from corner to corner, and also straight across from the four sides. All the threads will meet at the centre of the space, and, when they are in place, catch them at the centre by a knot made with the last thread, and begin to make the w h e e l. With the thread with which the knot was tied begin, close to the knot, and darn or weave around this k n o t, o v e r a n d under the foundation threads, each round of weaving increasing the diameter of the wheel or spider's web, until it has reached the desired size. Tack the thread underneath, then carry it to the edge of the open space and finish it off.

The wheel shown in illustration 15 is worked like No. 14, but when the plain wheel is finished the working thread is carried around at wider spaces, and knotted on each thread.

The wheel in illustration 16 has the foundation threads laid in the same manner as those already described, but all the threads, except the two diagonals running from corner to corner, are worked two by two with darning stitch, to form an eight-point star.

# Guest Towels.

The illustrations on this page are suggestions for ornamenting towels with crochet and cross-stitch. On the next page are clear working diagrams that will enable anyone to work the cross-stitch motifs.

WITH SHELL INSERTION.

The following are the directions for working the crochet insertions and edgings:—

WITH DEEP LACE EDGING.

## The Narrow Insertion.

Make a ch of 23 stitches; leave 8 ch and into each of the next 4 ch work 1 d c; ch 3, skip 3 ch, and into each of the next 4 ch work 1 d c; ch 3, leave 3 ch, and into last ch work 1 d c; ch 6 and turn.

*2nd Row.*—* 1 d c into first of 4 d c in first row; 3 ch, 4 d c over 3 ch in first row; 3 ch, 1 d c over last d c in first row; 3 ch, 1 d c into third ch at end; ch 6 and turn.

*3rd Row.*—4 d c over

second group of 3 ch; 3 ch, 4 d c over next 3 ch; ch 3, 1 d c into third ch at end; ch 6, turn and repeat from *.

## Deep Lace Edging.

This lace is worked in combination of d c and ch stitches, and since the open sp are worked one above the other, with the same number of ch between the d c stitches, the details of this working will not be given after the first rows. In every alternate row a V is formed by catching into the middle of the previous row. These V's will also be

WITH A NARROW INSERTION.

so designated after being once described in detail.

Make a ch of 54 stitches, turn and work 1 d c into the fifth ch from the needle and 1 into each of the next 6 ch. * Ch 5, 1 d c into next sixth stitch of the foundation ch ; repeat from * 5 times, making 6 large sp. Ch 2, 1 d c

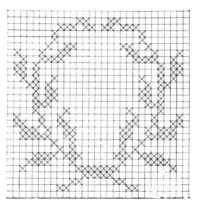

previous row. * This makes a V. Repeat from * to * 3 times. Make 6 d c in the next 6 ch stitches ; 2 ch, 1 s c in third ch ; 2 ch ; 7 d c in the 7 d c of previous row ; 9 ch, turn.

3rd Row.—Work 1 d c in the fifth ch from needle, 4 d c in the next 4 ch and 2 d c over the last 2 of the previous block of 7. Ch 5, 1 d c into last d c of previous block. Ch 5, 7 d c over the 7 d c of previous row. Finish the row with 4 large and 2 small sp ; ch 6, turn.

4th Row.—2 small sp, 3 V's, 19 d c, 1 V, 7 d c ; ch 9, turn.

5th Row.—7 d c, beginning in fifth ch from needle, 2 large sp, 19 d c over previous 19, 3 large and 2 small sp, turn.

6th Row.—2 small sp, 2

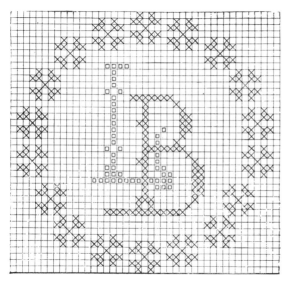

into third ch from last d c ; 2 ch, 1 d c into last ch of foundation, making 2 small sp. Ch 6, turn.

2nd Row.—Make 2 small sp by working 1 d c over the next to last d c of previous row ; 2 ch, 1 d c over next d c of previous row. * Ch 2, 1 s c into third stitch of 5 ch in previous row ; 2 ch, 1 d c over next d c of

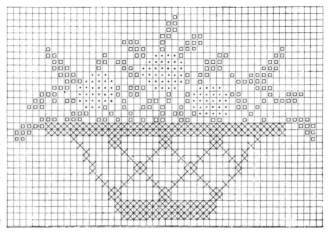

# Guest Towels.

V's, 13 d c, 1 large sp, 13 d c, 1 V, 7 d c; 9 ch, turn.

*7th Row.*—7 d c, 2 large sp, 7 d c, 1 large sp, 1 V, 1 large sp, 7 d c, 2 large 2 small sp.

*8th Row.*—2 small sp, 2 V's, 7 d c, 1 V, 1 large sp, 1 V, 7 d c, 2 V's, 7 d c; ch 4, turn. This is the middle of the scallop.

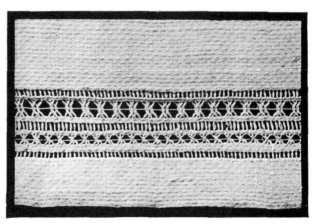

HEMSTITCHING AND DRAWN-THREAD WORK ARE MOST EFFECTIVE ON HUCKABACK.

*9th Row.*—6 d c, 2 large sp, 7 d c, 1 large sp, 1 V, 1 large sp, 7 d c, 2 large, 2 small sp.

*10th Row.*—2 small sp, 2 V's, 13 d c, 1 large sp, 13 d c, 1 V, 7 d c; 4 ch, turn.

*11th Row.*—6 d c, 2 large sp, 19 d c, 3 large 2 small sp, turn.

*12th Row.*—2 small sp, 3 V's, 19 d c, 1 V, 7 d c; 4 ch, turn.

*13th Row.*—6 d c, 2 large sp, 7 d c, 4 large 2 small sp, turn.

*14th Row.*—2 small sp, 4 V's, 7 d c, 1 V, 7 d c; 4 ch, turn.

*15th Row.*—6 d c, 6 large sp, 2 small sp, turn.

*16th Row.*—2 small sp, 5 V's, 7 d c, 9 ch, turn. The next row begins the second point, making the first of the block of d c in the fifth ch stitch from the needle. When the lace is of desired length, work loops of 9 ch, fastening each with a s c to the outer corner of each d c block. Crochet 9 s c over each of these ch loops.

## Shell Pattern Insertion.

Make a ch of 30 stitches, turn and into the fifth ch from the needle work 1 d c; ch 5, 1 s c into eleventh ch; ch 5, 1 s c into next sixth ch; ch 5, 1 s c into next sixth ch; ch 5, 1 d c into each of last 2 ch; ch 3, turn.

*2nd Row.*—1 d c into next to last one in first row; ch 3, 1 s c into third ch, 5 d c into s c on first row; 1 s c into third ch, 5 ch, 1 s c into third ch, 5 d c into next s c on first row, 1 s c into third ch; ch 3, 2 d c over last 2 in first row; ch 3 and turn.

*3rd Row.*—1 d c as before; 5 ch, 1 s c into third d c, 5 d c into next s c, 1 s c into third ch, 5 d c into next s c, 1 s c into third d c, 5 ch, 2 d c at end; ch 3 and turn.

*4th Row.*—1 d c, 3 ch, 1 s c into third ch, 5 ch, 1 s c into third d c, 5 d c into next s c, 1 s c into third d c; 5 ch, 1 s c into third ch; 3 ch, 2 d c at end; ch 3 and turn.

*5th Row.*—1 d c; 5 ch, 1 s c into third ch; 5 ch, 1 s c into third d c; 5 ch, 1 s c into third ch, 5 ch, 2 d c at end.

The second, third, fourth and fifth rows are repeated throughout.

78

# Stitches for Sports' Coats.

### Making a Coat in any Particular Style.

The following directions will be useful to those who want to make a sports' coat according to some particular style or shape. For this the first essential is a good paper pattern. Cut this out in tough brown paper, and avoid, as far as possible, creasing the pattern. Whatever wool be chosen, use a bone hook that will work the wool without splitting it, while making as fine a stitch as possible.

Always commence by making a chain long enough to fit the front edge of the pattern ; and after working the first row fit it on the pattern, as working into the ch stitches sometimes lengthens them. Work from the front to under the arm seam and shoulder, placing the crochet down on the paper pattern, and adding a stitch or decreasing one as required.

Commence the back portion down the centre, whether there is to be a seam there or not, as when one side is finished you break off the thread and join again to the centre ch and work the other side into the first, preserving the pattern.

Begin the sleeve at the inner seam, working the small gore at the top and bottom first on the length of ch, then

No. 1.—Long connected tr stitch, showing how the buttonholes are made.

No. 2.—The same stitch, showing how to narrow.

## Stitches for Sports' Coats.

No. 3.—A Stitch that will not sag.

work the main portion towards the back.

The collar and cuffs are often worked in a contrasting stitch, and these, too, are formed on the pattern.

Finish the lower edge of the coat, when the seams have been joined in the usual way, with Russian braid; and a neat finish is given to the inside by going over the edges with a row of d c worked with Peri-Lusta or Esplen D'or.

### Some Suitable Stitches.

These are all easily and quickly worked. The first is recommended for rapid and simple work, as it can so readily be narrowed to fit the pattern.

No. 5.—Purl Stitch.

A capital wool for a sports' coat is Faudel's Peacock Double Knitting Wool. You should be able to procure this from any Berlin Wool Repository, but if you experience any difficulty in this matter, write direct to Faudel's, Ltd., Newgate St., London.

### No. 1. Long Connected Treble Stitch.

Make the ch the required length, work a row of d c into the ch, turn, 4 ch, take up the third ch and draw the thread through, keeping the loop on the needle; do the same with the second and first ch, loop the thread through the first d c, this gives 5 loops on the needle, now work these off as

No. 4.—A Good Wearing Pattern.

in long tr, two at a time. It will be noticed that there are 3 upright bars across the long tr, hook the thread under each of these successively, and retain the loops on the needle, loop through next d c, then work off as before, and repeat. Every second row is d c, and both top portions of each stitch are taken up throughout. To form a buttonhole, cross over one of the long tr with 4 ch, on which the pattern is continued.

No. 6.—A Simple Pattern

To "narrow," take up two of the bars together, as shown in illustration No. 2.

### No. 3. A Stitch that will not Sag.

Commence with a row of d c into a ch, turn, 1 ch, 1 d c into each d c, taking up that portion of the stitch nearest to the thumb of the left hand.

1 ch to turn, d c into the first d c, taking up that portion of the stitch nearest to the forefinger of the left hand, 1 tr into the second loop of first row, * miss 1, 1 d c into next d c, miss a stitch in the first row, 1 tr into the next, and repeat from *.

The fourth row is the same as the second, and the fifth like the third, but place the tr between those of the third row. Then repeat these two rows.

### No. 4. A Good Wearing Pattern.

This is a single stitch in which the loops are drawn through the stitch below and the loop on the needle. This can only be worked on one side, and is very suitable for collar bands, facing, etc.

### No. 5. Purl Stitch.

This is also suitable for trimming, bands, belts, etc. Insert the hook from the back through the top portion of the stitch, and hook the thread through from the front, passing it through the loop on the needle at the same time.

### No. 6. A Simple Pattern.

Alternate rows of d c and tr, taking up both top portions of each stitch.

# Ideas for Table Cloths.

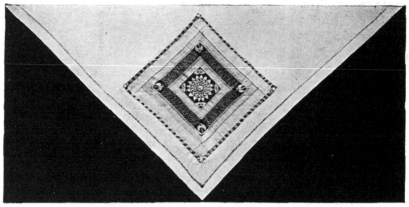

A drawn-thread work square inserted in the corner of a
hemstitched linen cloth. A Detail of this is on page 89.

Lace and damask combined in alternate squares will be a feature of the new five o'clock tea-cloths. The whole cloth may be made of these squares, or the lace can merely be introduced at the corners. This offers plenty of scope to the needleworker at home; fragments of lace and fragments of damask can be turned to account. It is desirable, however, that either the damask or the lace shall be of one pattern throughout, otherwise the cloth will look too much like patchwork. Linen or cambric could be used in place of the damask, in which case the lace must be of a lighter make.

Maltese lace is another new touch for household linen.

A pretty effect can be obtained by letting a drawnthread square, or any other piece of good needlework, into the corner of a cloth. This has much to recommend it. A small square can be handled more easily by the worker than the whole table-cloth ; moreover odd pieces of needlework can be preserved and utilised in this original way.

Lace and Damask are being combined in the fancy
tea-cloths of the season.

# A Lesson in Reticella Lace.

Reticella lace, which is also known as Greek point and sometimes as Venetian guipure, is one of the oldest known forms of needle work. It was made chiefly from the year 1480 to 1620, after which it was displaced by more elaborate and varied needlepoint and bobbin laces.

The first patterns consisted merely of simple outlines, worked over cords or threads left after others had been drawn or cut. Next in date came designs which showed outlines ornamented with crescents, triangles and circles, with, finally, intricate patterns, drawn on parchment, and worked out without any linen background or foundation. The rich dress of the sixteenth century did much to encourage the manufacture of reticella,

A CENTRE-PIECE.

3.—DETAIL OF FIGURES AT SIDES OF CENTRE-PIECE.

2.—DETAIL OF WORK AT CORNER OF CENTRE-PIECE.

but it was especially favoured for church purposes; bed and household linens were also elaborately decorated with this work.

Pattern books were costly and easily destroyed, so the various stitches and patterns were worked out on samplers or "sam-cloths," as they were then called; these being passed about or loaned among the different workers. The linen used for these samplers was of such tough fibre that much of it has lasted in good condition down to the present day, and many interesting pieces may be seen in museum collections.

Within the last quarter of a century, however, interest in the original reticella has been renewed, and schools and classes have been formed

# Reticella
# Lace.

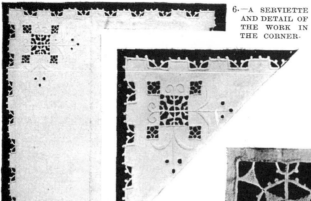

6.—A SERVIETTE AND DETAIL OF THE WORK IN THE CORNER.

are pictured, one of them matching the centre in design and border, the second (illustration 5) being rather more simple in design. Illustration 6 shows a serviette about twelve inches square, and an enlarged detail illustration of the work in the corner of the serviette. Illustration 7 shows a corner in another design.

12.—SIMPLE SQUARE OF WOVEN BARS AND PYRAMIDS.

in Italy, in which young girls are taught to copy the stitchery of long ago. So far as durability is concerned, there is no form of needlework that can in any way compare with it, and though many people interested in needlework may hesitate to undertake a piece of reticella, once attempted, one cannot help being fascinated, there is such variety in the stitchery.

The materials required are not expensive, for the linen is wide and cuts to good advantage, and the thread, whether bought by the spool or skein, costs but a few pence. A pure, round-thread linen must be selected, of rather heavy quality, but not too closely woven ; the size of the working thread depends largely, of course, on the texture of the background.

The first illustration shows a centrepiece, thirty inches square, and other illustrations show enlarged details of the openwork figures at the corners and sides. Two round plate d'oileys

13.—SQUARE WITH WHIPPED BARS, BUTTONHOLE STITCH AND PICOTS.

The preliminary work, that is, the preparing of the squares or openings for the stitchery, is done in much the same manner as for Danish cut-work, and anyone familiar with the latter embroidery will have little difficulty in making reticella lace. The outlines of the openings must be run, then slashed through the centre from corner to corner if it is

15.—WHIPPED BARS AND PYRAMIDS FORMING A STAR.

a square, more frequently if a circular figure is to be made ; these edges are then turned back smoothly to the wrong side and afterwards the folded edge is either closely overhanded or button-holed. This finished, baste the linen down on a piece of American cloth, being careful to keep the lines of the

11.—BULLION-STITCH PICOT IN EDGE OF SERVIETTE.

9, 10.—COMPLETED SQUARE AND METHOD OF WORKING.

opening perfectly true, and taking the basting stitches close enough together to prevent any slipping or pulling out of shape when the filling-in stitchery is done.

At first glance it may be remarked that this latter also resembles hedebo work, but a closer examination will reveal the fact that reticella has a few distinctive features which are all its own. These are notably the whipped bars or cords,  the woven bars, picot-edged points, and the simple tracery of flat satin-stitch, which usually either surrounds or is worked above and below the open figures.

The method for working both the whipped and woven bars is clearly detailed in illustrations 7 and 8. For the former lay two threads straight across from side to side, then bring a third thread up to the centre, twist

once around here to fasten, and lay two threads at right angles ; then if the figure requires it, lay two more groups of threads across diagonally, from corner to corner. When this is finished, carry the thread, without breaking, down beside one of the bars, fasten in the linen and then overhand over the three threads back to the centre, laying the stitches as close to-gether as possible without overlapping. Repeat for the next half bar, and continue in this way until the foundation is completed, whipping back to the linen on the bar which was first laid. The woven bars are made in the same manner except that four threads must be

7.—ANOTHER DESIGN FOR A SERVIETTE CORNER, WITH DETAIL SHOWING METHOD OF WORKING.

# Reticella Lace.

laid, and, instead of being overcast, they are woven, under and over two threads, back and forth until the bar is finished ; this is seen in illustration 7.

Practically all designs or figures use a central wheel or ring, and this is made by twisting s thread twice around, catching it into every bar, then buttonholing over this double thread, putting in a picot wherever indicated. Picots may be made in any one of the three following ways ; first, a single loop picot made by placing a needle or pin in the American cloth about a sixteenth of an inch below the bar being made, winding the thread once around this to form a loop, fastening it by taking

17.—SQUARE WITH SATIN STITCH.

one buttonhole stitch around the loop close up to the bar; this method is shown in illustration 9. The second method is with the roll or bullion-stitch, as shown in the detail of the edge, at illustration 11. For the third method, make a single loop around a needle in the same manner as directed for the first picot, but instead

8.— BEGINNING THE SQUARE, OVERCAST EDGES AND WHIPPED BARS.

of fastening, wind the thread once more around the needle, and then buttonhole over the two threads back to the bar, pushing the first stitch as close down to the needle as possible.

The figure which forms the centre of the square in each corner of the large centre-piece, has no foundation bars, the points in the corners of the square being first made, then one point in the centre of each side. After these are completed the centre wheel is begun. This latter is made in the hand by winding the thread ten or twelve times around the top of a thimble to form a ring, covering this ring with close buttonholing. When this is finished, work a row of loose buttonhole loops around the edge at regular intervals, then twist back across the top of these loops and work another row of close buttonholing. Now baste the ring to the American cloth in the centre of the square and proceed to work the four points opposite the corner points already made, not forgetting to join the points together by the finely-whipped bars seen in the illustration.

These are worked while the point is being made and on the same place as the foundation bars previously described.

16.—SQUARE WITH SATIN STITCH.

The small square which is seen twice on each side of the centre-piece is used as the centre figure in the corner of the serviette at illustration 6. Woven bars form the foundation for this design, the points and semi-circles being done after the bars are completed. The figure used in the second serviette corner is shown partially worked in the detail at illustration 7. From this illustration it is easy to see the plan or method followed; the difference between the hedebo points and those used in reticella should not fail to be noted. In the former the buttonhole loops are left a little loose, but in the latter they should be pulled as close as possible, so that the finished points will appear almost solid. In both cases the actual stitchery is the same. Each row of buttonholing contains one stitch less than the preceding row, until only 1 stitch

14.—ELABORATE SQUARE WITH
WOVEN BARS AND PYRAMIDS.

4.—SMALL D'OILEY WITH BORDER MATCHING
CENTRE-PIECE.

5.—PLATE D'OILEY IN SIMPLE DESIGN.

remains to complete the point. At the end of each buttonholed row the thread is carried back to the beginning of the row, by oversewing or whipping into the top of each buttonhole stitch. Unless the point is to be connected with some other figure, the thread is carried back to the linen edge again by whipping or oversewing along the side of the pyramid or point.

The treatment of the edge of the centre-piece, d'oileys and serviette, is most appropriate, the quaint button-holed and picot-edged scallops adding much to the beauty of each piece. In making either edge the outline must be first run with a fine, uneven stitch, then the buttonholing is begun and worked as shown in the detail. The loose loops are worked over three threads with a roll or bullion stitch picot in the centre of each loop. In cutting the linen away beyond this buttonholed edge, be most careful not to snip the loose loops or back of the buttonhole stitches, for if this should occur the edge is practically ruined, it being almost impossible to repair the damage satisfactorily.

After all the reticella figures are finished, the eyelets should be worked. To be correct and in keeping with the rest of the work the latter should be done with linen thread and have no underlaying or padding, the stitches being laid perfectly straight and not sloped or slanted to conform to the shape of the figure.

With the knowledge of the general method of working, any design may readily be copied, and the field of original design, through varying the combination of the figures, is unlimited. A number of squares are shown, any one of which may be copied exactly or modified to suit the worker. Illustration 12 represents a square with woven bars, like those in illustration 7, crossing from the straight sides only. The small half-circles at each side may be worked before the centre is begun, but the points or pyramids at each corner should not be made until the centre is completed; each point is then attached to the large buttonholed circle, after which the thread is carried, by oversewing along the side of the pyramid, to the edge of the linen, where it may be fastened off invisibly.

The square shown in illustration 13, is particularly lace-like in appearance and does not employ the usual pyramid forms, though the half-circles at the corners are a feature to be noted, as are also the small circles, formed on each of the whipped bars.

The large figure that connects all these bars is more square than circular in shape, and, as may be plainly seen, is composed of spaced buttonholing on a foundation of solid buttonhole stitch; the half-circles in the corners are worked in the same manner.

Illustration 14 might be called an elaboration of illustration 12, though it has some points of dissimilarity, noticeably the omission of the circle enclosing the central pyramids. The bars are woven, and cross from the sides only. Whether the central pyramids or those at the corners shall be made first is entirely optional with the worker. The usual rule, when a pyramid is to be attached to another figure, is to make the joining with the thread from the point of the pyramid, where the one buttonhole stitch completes it; but when two pyramids are to be connected, as in this case, the worker may consult her own fancy or convenience.

There is one consideration that is of importance in all of these squares, and that is, that all sides shall be made symmetrical. The distance from the centre, for instance, at which the foundation threads for the buttonholing are caught into the woven bars, must be exactly the same on each of the four bars, else the figure when completed will be uneven; the balance on all four sides must be carefully maintained. In this square (illustration 14) there are five points on each half of each woven bar where another section of the figure is joined to the bar, and the correct spacing is most important. A truth apparent here is applicable to every kind of needlework—care and accuracy when one is learning will bear good results in the future in making the correct methods come to one's fingers mechanically.

The square seen in illustration 15 is larger, but not quite so elaborate as the others. In this respect it is an apt illustration of the decorative value of the picots—it is really their absence that makes the work, in this instance, look so plain. The foundation bars are whipped, but the circle surrounding the centre and the loops worked on this circle are in buttonhole stitch, as are also the bars crossing the corners and the loops worked upon them. In contrast to most of the other squares, the centre of this is worked solid in a raised or relief wheel or "spider." In the ordinary wheel the thread is woven around under one of the "spokes"

that radiate from the centre and over the next, alternating in this way until the wheel was the required size. Whether the number of radiating threads is even or uneven is of no importance in making a relief wheel. The thread is passed around each bar, that is, the needle is passed under it, then under it again, as if taking a back stitch; at the second stitch the needle continues under the next bar. The last two illustrations (Nos. 16 and 17) are extremely simple squares, used in conjunction with flat, satin-stitch embroidery. The first square is crossed diagonally by whipped bars. The small, flower-like figure at the centre-crossing of these bars is composed of four bullion-stitch picots.

A DRAWN-THREAD SQUARE WORKED BY A
CHINESE GIRL IN MALAYSIA.

# Smocking.

"Smocking" is much in vogue for decorating the necks of children's frocks, sleeves, etc., and for aprons, blouse yokes and cuffs. There are a great many designs for this method of ornamenting the gatherings but they are all formed on the same principle. Sometimes fancy headings in stitchery are employed to still further enhance the work, and Fig. 1 shows three of the most usual stitches for the purpose, with the plain outlining stitch at the top. This is often used in lines at each side of the head-

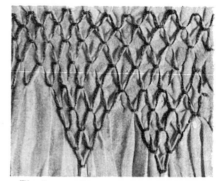

Fig. 3,—MAKING POINTS AND SCALLOPS.

makes the work very easy to do, and even in appearance.

The smocking is done from right to left and stout mercerised cotton, such as Ardern's No. 8 "Sylko," is suitable. Commence by slipping the needle under two gathers, draw out the thread and form another stitch over the two edges, about a quarter of an inch above this stitch take up the last of the two gathers below and the following one, insert the needle through from right to left and make the stitch over the two edges, now descend to the first line and take the last of these two with the following gather and secure in the same way.

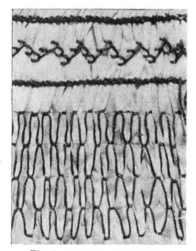

Fig. 1.—SHOWING A FEATHER-STITCHED HEADING.

ing and at the sides of strips worked up as insertions.

Fig. 2 shows the smocking stitch and the way in which the material is arranged. Prepare the material and make the rows of gathers where the smocking is to begin. It is absolutely necessary that the gathers be very even and that the stitches in the rows are all in line. To ensure this, lines can, where possible, be marked on the back of the material, or threads may be drawn to mark both horizontal and upright lines. The latter

This is the entire smocking stitch which is varied in a number of ways but is always quite simple and easy to work.

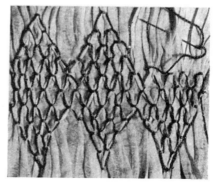

Fig. 4.—SMOCKING DONE IN DIAMONDS.

The second row is made at the same distance from the first row as the lines are apart, and where the thread is carried up to the connecting stitch in the preceding row you do not make the back stitch over the edge, you simply run the thread behind the stitches already there.

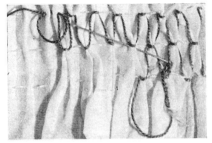

Fig. 2.—SHOWING HOW THE WORK IS DONE.

In making scallops as in Fig. 3 the rows are worked for the scallop to and fro without breaking the thread and

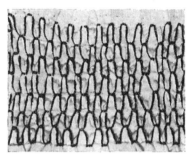

Fig. 5.—PLAIN SMOCKING AS SEEN ON CHILDREN'S PINAFORES.

the work must be turned in the hand so as to bring the beginning of the row to the right. When the smocking is finished the running threads are pulled out.

All knots on the thread must be kept on the back.

Fig. 4 shows the smocking done in diamonds, this being the scallop

worked evenly at both sides of a plain row.

Fig. 5 is a sample of plain smocking as usually employed on children's frocks, pinafores, etc.

Fig. 1 is a sample of the smocking with a fancy heading. The outline stitch is used at each side of the feather-stitching, and of course these lines are worked over rows of gatherings of which there must be as many as there are lines in the design, including the heading.

In arranging the gatherings any seams that occur in the garment must be kept between the pleats in order that they may not shew on the smocking, and care must be taken to fasten off all the ends of the threads securely.

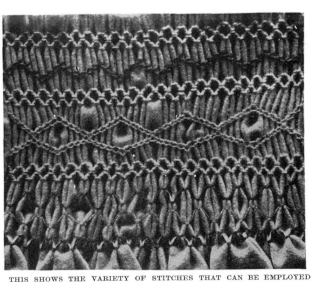

THIS SHOWS THE VARIETY OF STITCHES THAT CAN BE EMPLOYED AND THE PRETTY EFFECTS THAT CAN BE OBTAINED BY THE ADDITION OF FEATHER-STITCHING,

# Herring=bone Embroidery.

Fig. 1.—SHOWING THREE STAGES OF STITCHES.

Herring-bone embroidery has been very much in evidence lately for dress trimming, scarfs, etc., but it is only now that it is coming into vogue for trimming table and bedroom napery. With its brilliant tints and strong contrasts it is very striking, and when the colours are judiciously combined, it makes a very beautiful and cheerful-looking ornamentation. For napery for the afternoon tea-service the tints of the colouring on the china tea-set

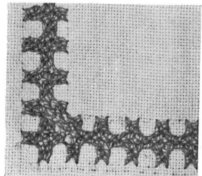

Fig. 2.—THE STITCHES FINISHED.

Fig. 4.—THE FOUNDATION FOR THIS BORDER.

should be matched as nearly as possible with the threads employed; and the same with the toilet service when making dressing-table cover and d'oileys.

One form of the embroidery, the inter-lacing stitch, is very largely used for this purpose, and if the intricacies of the first stitch be thoroughly mastered, the work can be done very quickly, and any amount of designs for d'oiley borders, table centres, tea-cloth borders, etc., can be

Fig. 3.—FILLING IN THE STITCHES.

92

arranged from the Maltese cross into which this stitch evolves.

The stitch itself is formed on a foundation of other stitches somewhat like the herring-bone stitch.

Fig. 1 shows three stages of the stitch. The first is the large herringbone with equal spaces above and below through which a second row is worked with the slanting stitches crossing exactly in the middle. Great care must be taken to have the stitches correctly crossing each other ; where a stitch is above, the one below it must go under the following stitch.

By studying Fig. 1 carefully, the principle involved can easily be seen. It does not matter which end the interlacing is commenced at so long as the thread is carried under and over the alternate stitches. Only one half of the interlacing is shown in Fig. 1 ; the upper half is done in the same way exactly. Of course, to do the foundation stitches evenly, the lines in the material must be followed; or if this is not possible on account of fineness, then lines must be drawn as a guide, and for round d'oileys these can readily be marked in with a compass.

Fig. 2 shows the stitches finished, and gives you an idea how the corner is worked. It will be seen that each finished stitch takes the form of a small cross, and this principle is carried out in the variation of the design as shown in Fig. 3. Here we have four of the stitches forming a larger Maltese cross to elaborate the border.

Fig. 4 shows the foundation for this border. The large crosses can be worked at both sides of the row of straight stitches if liked and various colours introduced into the design.

This work is very effective when done on a coarse make of linen, with mercerised cotton matching the threads of the material in coarseness.

For towel ends it is peculiarly well adapted, and looks very well worked with crimson or a dull blue of No. 5 "Star Sylko."

It will be well to remember that the evenness of the interlacing depends upon the foundation being properly done, and it must be borne in mind, as will readily be seen from Fig. 1, that all the slanting stitches in the first row go over or under at opposite ends of the row, the slanting stitches going in the other direction. In the first row, when a stitch is over at the top it must be over at the bottom also ; this is ensured by slipping the needle under the thread where necessary ; then in the second row the thread which is over in the first is under in this row, and *vice versâ* If this be remembered the stitch is quite easy to accomplish.

A Pretty
Butterfly Design
in Cross-stitch.

Notice the effective use of single uncrossed stitches.

# Hardanger Embroidery.

Fig. 3.

This pretty form of needlework takes its name from the town of Hardanger, in Norway. It is very easy to work and effective in appearance. Insertion, collars, blouse trimmings can all be easily worked into the coarse linen fabrics so fashionable during the summer; then the number of household uses to

Fig. 1.

which it is applicable is almost unlimited.

Special canvas and linen material are sold for this purpose, and of these the best quality should always be chosen.

The threads usually employed are stout Peri-Lusta for the outlining and a fine linen thread for the weaving.

Fig. 1 shows the simple outline stitch worked on a square with the threads being drawn ready for working.

Fig. 2 shows

Fig. 2.

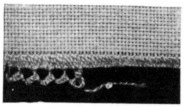

Fig. 5.

the method of weaving the bars, of which there are a variety, also the picot at each side of a bar and one in the process of making.

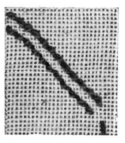

Fig. 4.

By looking at the position of the needle and carefully noting the manner in which the thread is twisted around it this can readily be manipulated. Pull the thread through somewhat after the manner of a French knot, then slip the needle through the bars and form another at the opposite side.

Fig. 3 shows how small squares are formed.

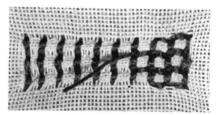

Fig. 6.

Fig. 4 is the back-stitching often used in double rows to embellish the design. Both these are worked together, crossing the needle to the opposite row alternately, on the back.

Always finish off the thread on the side of a square farthest from the centre, and when beginning a square be careful to have the knot of the thread on the same

Fig. 7.

Fig. 8 is a design suitable for window hangings as a border over a two inch hem-stitched hem, or it may be applied to a table or afternoon tea-cloth.

Fig. 9 shows the corner for Fig. 8.

Fig. 10 is a pretty design for a stock collar into which the "Punched" embroidery is introduced.

All these are very easily worked from the details and with a little care can be made side, in order that it may not show on the right side through the bars.

The work is usually finished with a row of buttonhole stitching as in Fig. 5, and sometimes the little open-work edge also shown in the figure is added to give a lacy appearance. This can readily be copied from the illustration.

Fig. 6 shows the open stitch used in the design for the stock collar shown in Fig. 10. This stitch is the same as that used for the "Punched" embroidery.

Fig. 7 is a pretty and bold design for a table-cloth border. This may be worked in colours, and looks very well in crimson on an ecru linen, also in delf blue on white or cream linen.

up into various articles. Use only a very sharp scissors, and be very careful to cut only the threads required. The outlining should all be complete before attempting to cut any of the threads, and it is best to cut only a little of the threads at a time, one square will be sufficient,

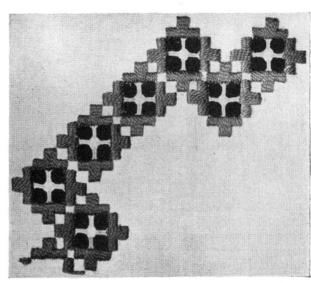

Fig. 9.  A PRETTY CORNER.

then when this is complete with all bars filled in proceed to the next.

The number of threads cut should always be even on account of having to be equally divided for the bars.

Fig. 10.

In the curtain border a little lace stitch is used to fill in the squares. This is only a simple button-hole stitch taken into each of the four sides during the process of working the bar.

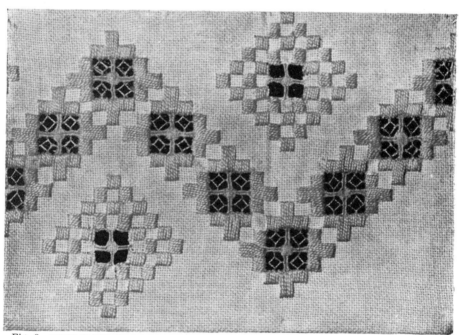

Fig. 8. TABLE-CLOTH OR WINDOW CURTAIN BORDER.

### Needlepoints.

Do not patch worn linen—either personal or household — with new material; otherwise the strong new patch may tear away the older stuff.

Never join material that has been cut on the cross to material that has been cut on the straight; like should always be joined to like.

In mending, see that the threads of a patch run the same way as those of the material it is placed upon, otherwise there will be puckers.

# A Lesson in Macramé Work.

This work is being revived at the present time, and all sorts of pretty little bags, insertions, furniture laces, and fringes are to be seen made of it.

This work is done by knotting, tying or plaiting a number of threads together to form any particular design. Its great

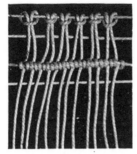

Fig. 2.—SHOWING THE STITCHES.

durability, and the number of uses to which it can be applied, make it well worth one's while to devote the little time and attention necessary to master the different knots and stitches used.

The materials necessary are the thread or macramé twine, a crochet-hook, a sharp scissors, and the cushion.

The cushion is easily made by obtaining a small box about 18 inches long, 6 inches deep, and 10 inches wide. This is a handy size, but smaller

Fig. 3.—THE DRAWSTRING.

may be used for little pieces of work, and indeed the cushion can easily be dispensed with for these if a pair of clamps with any kind of an appliance on top to which the thread can be fastened is to be had. For all purposes it is better to have the cushion, however.

Having procured the box, remove the lid and knock out the front, round off the two top corners and make them equal. See that the seams are all close and secure. Now fill the

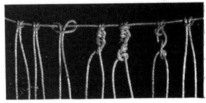

Fig. 1.—THE CORD, AND METHOD OF KNOTTING.

box up to the level of the top with horse-hair, if to be had, or cotton wadding, or other filling stuff; tack a covering of green linen closely and evenly along the back edge of the top, turning in the sides neatly; tack all round the edges, putting in more padding to make the cushion even and very firm. The edges can be neatened with a row of brass-headed tacks put in all round the linen about an inch apart, and of course the wood-work can be stained, or painted and varnished, to complete

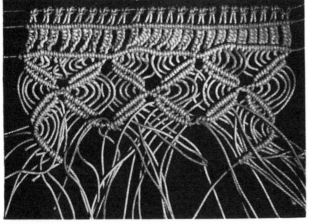

SHOWING THE WORK IN PROGRESS.

## A Macramé Insertion.

the work. On the sides, about 3 and 6 inches from the back, screw in a couple of rings, such as are used for pictures, on which to tie the foundation strings, technically termed "cords." A packet of pins with glass bead heads will be required if the work contains picots.

As the stitches and knots used are many, we will confine our attention in this lesson to the stitches required for making the little bag illustrated on page 99.

For this bag you will require a ball of fine macramé twine, any colour liked. For each dia-

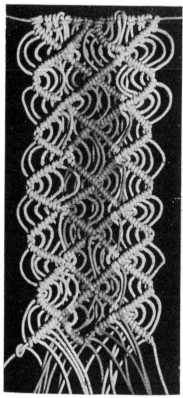

Fig. 4.—A SIMPLE INSERTION IN TWO COLOURS.

mond in the design you will require 16 threads, and there are 9 diamonds in a row, therefore 144 threads. The threads are put in doubled, and as they must be cut twice as long, at least, as the piece of work, the threads are cut in this instance one yard long, giving half a yard for each. From the ball of twine cut 72 yard lengths, arrange a double cord from one side of the cushion to the other, and have this very securely fastened to the screws.

Fig. 1 shows the "cord" and the method of knotting on the thread.

Fold the thread in two and take hold of the centre loop, put this downwards behind the "cord," insert the ends through the loop and pull up the knot tight. Do this with each

of the 72 threads, and have them close together.

Tie another cord to the screws over the threads and immediately below the knots, take up the first thread and insert it to the left down behind the "cord" and through the loop made by the thread; now repeat to the right, so that you have the vertical thread behind between two knots, repeat with each thread, and keep the row of knots close up to the first row.

There is a row of vertical bars after the knot stitches; each bar is formed thus: Take up a thread and form 6 plain buttonhole stitches over it with the thread to the right. Repeat with every 2 threads. You now fasten another "cord" to the left side of the cushion and catch hold of the end with the right hand; keep this cord up to the buttonhole stitches, and with the left hand form another row of double knots exactly like the second row. See that the buttonhole stitches all lie in the same direction, and pull the "cord" to make it even with that at the other side of the bars.

Fig. 2 shows the stitches clearly.

Always finish a row before commencing the next, as this ensures even work.

The diamonds are formed of the knot stitch in double rows slanting from right to left alternately. Each bar of knots is formed on 8 threads. Take the first thread in the right hand, and with the left form the double knot with the second thread ; hold the thread in the right hand, which now becomes a "cord" as the stitches are formed on it, in a slightly downward sloping direction ; make the knots with each of the remainder of 8 threads in succession. Leave the "cord" and commence at the beginning of this bar again ; take up the first "cord" now (this was the second thread before the first row was formed), and, holding it in the right hand as before, work the second row of knots over it close up to the first row and form the last 2 knots with the 'cord' of the 1st row.

On the next 8 threads you reverse these movements, starting with the eighth as a "cord," and holding it in the left hand while you form the stitches with the right. The bars are tied closely together where they meet with the last 'cords' in a double knot.

A little practice will enable anyone to form these bars with speed and accuracy.

The rows worked in this way completes the bag, which is now removed from the cushion and the sides neatly joined with the twine. At the lower end the threads are cut away about a ¼-inch from the last bar, the ends are turned in and neatly and securely sewn behind the bars with stout linen thread of the same shade as the bag.

The end is finished with 5 tassels run through 2 points at opposite sides, and so closing this end. Each tassel has a loop at the top for the purpose of attaching it to the bag; this loop is formed of 20 ch stitches made with the macramé twine ; the ends are knotted and form the tie for the tassel.

Fig. 3 shows how to make the drawstring. This is formed of a length of the twine doubled to form 2 double cords, and each of them is formed into a single knot over the other alternately. Insert one cord

THE COMPLETED BAG.

at each side and finish the ends with a tassel.

Fig. 4 shows a very simple insertion that can easily be worked from the foregoing directions. It is worked in 2 colours, and as this is formed on the width very long threads are required. There are 12 sets of threads, 4 at each side in the same colour and 4 in the centre of a contrasting shade. Single knotted bars only are used, and each group of 4 threads is taken up with a bar.

This design forms a nice heading for the deep fringes now so fashionable, and any colour threads may be used.

# A Lesson in Hedebo Work.

The centre-piece which is illustrated on the next page is a wonderfully good specimen of Hedebo embroidery (or Danish cut-work, as it is also called), and though at first glance one

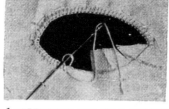
1.—PREPARING THE OPEN FIGURES

would be apt to see only the elaborateness of the work and the unusual variety in the number of stitches used, a closer examination of the piece will be sure to result in the conviction that, after all, it lies quite within the capability of the average deft needlewoman.

It is, of course, obvious that Danish cut-work is not to be ranked with those kinds of embroidery which can be worked rapidly, and which, more often than not, wear out just as rapidly. On the contrary, the beginner will be almost sure to find that the work progresses but slowly, especially at first, but people who are familiar with the Hedebo work speak of it as "the embroidery which never wears out." It is certainly true that

THE SMALL FIGURE IN CENTRE-PIECE.

if proper materials are used and the work is well done, its wearing properties are almost endless; therefore, bearing these facts in mind, one need not hesitate in undertaking a piece of this fascinating embroidery, more particularly as the cost of the materials is not at all high.

A good round-thread linen for the background is a necessity, but apart from this the linen thread, which is used for all of the buttonholing, and also in making the stitches which fill the open spaces, does not cost much, while the mercerised cotton for the solid embroidery is still cheaper. The weight or size of the thread used for the buttonholing depends to a great extent on the quality of the linen background, but to choose too fine a thread is a mistake. No. 60 is a good size to select for ordinary linen, while if mercerised cotton is used for the satin-stitch work, choose No. 25 or 30.

The old pieces of

2.—A SIMPLE FILLING STITCH.

Hedebo always show the satin-stitch done with linen thread, the stitches being taken on the diagonal and the figures worked flat without any padding. Many of the modern workers, however, employ mercerised cotton,

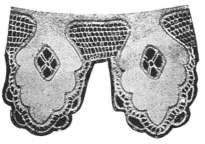

A SECTION OF THE EDGE OF THE
LARGE CENTRE-PIECE.

as producing a smoother and more satiny finish, and some of them do not hesitate to raise the figures slightly with rows of padding.

The underlying principle and foundation stitch in Danish cut-work

is buttonhole stitch. Examine all the detail illustrations to this article, and you will see that all the seemingly intricate figures are formed practically of this stitch alone, which by being worked close or open, or by simply changing the size of the stitch itself, produces a wonderful variety of effect.

In detail figure 1, the proper way to prepare the open figures for the filling stitch is shown. Begin by

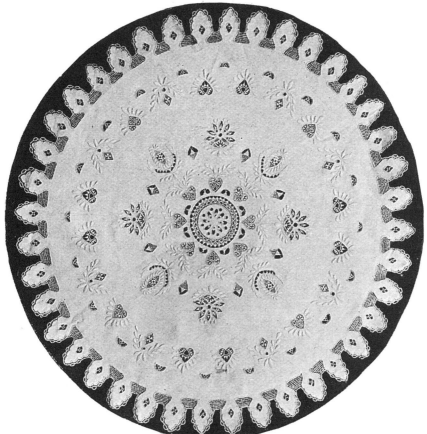

A CENTRE-PIECE IN DANISH CUT-WORK OR
HEDEBO EMBROIDERY.

running the outline with a rather fine, uneven

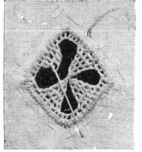

FIGURE 3.

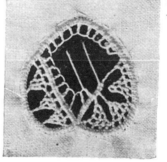

FIGURE 4.

buttonholing, in that the work is done from left to

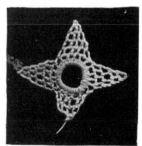

FIGURE 5.

FIGURE 8.

FIGURE 7.

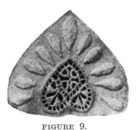

FIGURE 9.

darning-stitch; after this is finished, cut a slit through the centre from end to end, another crosswise from side to side, and then cut the pieces thus formed as many times as is necessary to enable one to fold them back smoothly to the wrong side, on the run outline. Figures with square sides will not need to be cut or snipped, except at the corners, while those that are curved must be cut several times between corners.

The figure is then ready to be buttonholed, and it will be seen, by referring to the detail given, that the stitch differs somewhat from ordinary

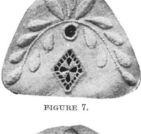

DETAIL FIGURE 6.

DETAIL FIGURE 10.

right, and the needle placed as shown in the illustration. This method raises the edge or back of the stitch a trifle, and, especially in the open or loose button-holing, produces a much prettier effect than if done in the regular way.

After the buttonholed edge is completed, the edges of the linen which project beyond it on the wrong side may be clipped off close, without fear of fraying, and the linen basted on a piece of black or dark green American cloth. Do not stint this basting; take the stitches close together, so that when the filling stitches are worked, the shape or outline of the figure will not be altered. Where there are a number of small figures grouped together to form one large one, as in detail fig. 6, or when two figures lie fairly close together, one piece of American cloth may be used under the entire group or groups, but generally speaking, it is not wise to attempt to use too large a piece, as it makes the work awkward to handle.

After the American cloth is firmly basted in place, the figure is ready for the filling stitch. Detail figure 2 shows a pretty simple stitch made in

AN ENLARGED DETAIL OF THE CENTRE MOTIF.

A D'OILEY TO GO WITH THE CENTRE-PIECE.

the following manner :—Begin at the left side, holding the curved edge towards you, and work a row of loose buttonhole stitches around to the opposite side. Whip or overhand back to the beginning, taking one stitch in each space, then fasten thread. This last can best be done by taking a few tiny back stitches in between the rows of buttonhole stitches which finish the edge of the linen. Next turn the figure round, so that the straight side or lower edge is toward you, and after fastening the thread firmly at a point a little less than one-quarter the distance across, take a stitch in the centre, leaving a loose loop. Twist back on this thread to the beginning, then buttonhole across it; make a second loop next to it in the same way. When this second loop is buttonholed half-way across, begin the third loop, by taking a stitch back into the centre of the first one and, after twisting back and forth, cover it with buttonholing, in the same way as the first two. Take a couple of stitches at the centre through the loops or row of holes on the curved side, in order to hold the top loop in place. When it is finished, complete the second half of the second loop.

It is seldom, if ever, that one sees a piece of Danish cut-work that does not make frequent use of the button-hole points or triangles, which may be employed singly or in connection with other stitches to equally good advantage. Detail figure 7 is a diamond-shaped figure which is filled with a Maltese cross made of four of the points just mentioned, and detail figure 3 clearly portrays the working plan. A row of the open buttonhole stitches or squares, the same as were made on the curved side of figure 2, is worked all around the edge of the diamond, but instead of whipping all the way back on these squares, over-hand one side to within two or three stitches of the corner, then turn and work a row of five holes, as the beginning of the first point. Whip back on these five stitches, make another row, taking a stitch into each hole, and continue whipping back and working rows of buttonhole stitches, until there is only one stitch left; then whip down the left side of the point. Continue overcasting or

whipping across the top of the first row of holes until the place for the next point is reached. When the last or single stitch on the third point is reached, join it to the tip of the first point; join the second and fourth points together when finishing the latter.

Figures 8 and 9 show different arrangements of these same points, and it may not be amiss to explain the working of each figure in detail. The heart-shaped opening, figure 4, shows one side worked like figure 8, with the second side like figure 9, the lower portion showing the beginning of the row of open squares which outline the lower part of figure 9.

In working figure 8, begin by stretching a bar of thread from the centre of the upper part of the heart, diagonally across to the side, twisting back on it in the usual way. On this bar work a row of loose buttonhole loops, and in whipping back, work the three points, fastening the tip of each to the side of the heart, and whip down the side to the bar to start the next point. Then work a row of buttonholing on the lower side of the twisted bar, letting the back of the buttonhole come on the side nearest the lower part of the heart. Repeat this figure on the second side, and when the last row of buttonholing is a little less than half done, begin the figure which is to fill the rest of the open space, by stretching a bar across to the first side, working the row of loose buttonhole stitches, then the points, and lastly the row of close buttonholing. When the latter is completed, return to the second side and finish buttonholing that bar.

Figure 9 shows the row of open squares worked first on the two side portions, making the three points when whipping back. Then stretch a thread from the centre, diagonally across to the side, and after having twisted back on it, cover with a row of close buttonhole stitches, catching in the tips of the points as shown in detail illustration 4. When the side portions are completed, work a row of open squares all the way around the four sides of the open space, making the loops at the points somewhat longer than at the sides, in order to make the centre opening square. In whipping back, make a buttonholed loop in the centre of each side, joining them together by bars of twisted thread. Finish the figure by covering the top of the open squares with a row of close buttonhole stitches.

The band of openwork or lace which is set in the middle of the centre-piece, as well as the medallion in the centre of the d'oiley, is made by hand, and undoubtedly they do entail considerable work, but they could be omitted and the linen left plain without lessening the attractiveness of either piece. The centre star in the d'oiley is made on the same plan as the star in the centre of figure 10, which is shown again partly worked at figure 5. Begin by winding the thread ten times over a pencil; cover the ring thus made with close buttonhole stitches, and then begin the points, being careful to space them evenly. When the latter are finished, baste the star in position on the American cloth and continue working the rest of the figure.

As illustrated the centre-piece measures thirty inches in diameter, but should one prefer a smaller piece it would be a simple matter to omit the entire outer band of cut-work, stamping a scallop about three inches beyond the inner band.

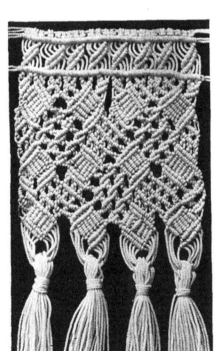
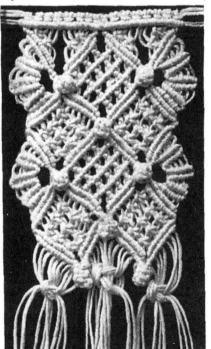

Two new designs for Macramé Borders.

# Macramé Edgings.

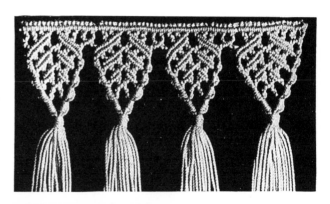

The Edging on the right would be suitable for Blinds or for finishing the edges of woodwork shelves.

This is a deeper edge, worked with rather coarser thread. It could be used in various ways for household decoration.

This Design would make a good Mantel Border, and contains some of the stitches already described. Strutt's Macramé Twine is the best thread to use for this work.

# Darned Filet Crochet.

Darned filet crochet is a very pretty variation of the darned netting that was so popular with the last generation. It may be said to be a compromise between the darned netting and the filet crochet designs that are now so much in vogue. It consists of

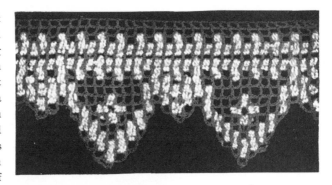

If the mesh is in cream cotton and the darning in white cotton, the effect is good.

A pretty effect has been obtained in the second illustration by the use of long stitches, and the cotton being given an extra loop round outside the darned meshes.

a strip of plain filet crochet, open mesh, whatever width and length is desired. The pattern is then woven in and out with a darning needle and mercerised thread, as in the darned netting.

The third illustration shows a simple insertion that could easily be copied.

Though the foundations of the designs shown on this page look dark, it is merely to throw up the darning. This work wears very well, and can be used in many ways.

# Point Lace Braid Collar.

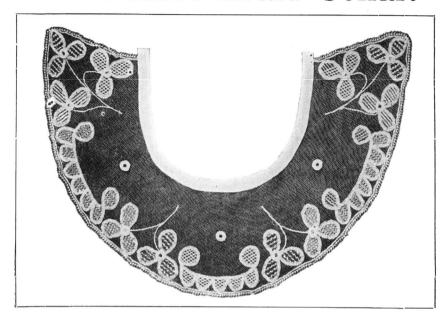

For this collar, procure a small piece of the best fine net, some yards of the narrowest point lace braid and a skein of embroidery cotton of the mercerised kind, medium fine, with 1 yard of pearl edging for the bordering.

Copy the design, which is very simple, in single lines on a piece of stiff white paper with pen and ink, or draw it in sections on separate pieces of paper, then transfer to the piece intended for use. Allow a small margin around the collar shape and tack the net smoothly over the design, tacking all round the lines so that the net cannot pull away.

Commencing at the left side, tack the braid through the centre all over the lines through the paper, keeping the outer sdge of the braid level with the outline. When all the lines have been covered except the stems in the clover motif, sew the outer edge of the braid to the net with very fine sewing cotton, using neat "top" stitching, and taking care not to go through the paper while picking up the meshes in the net.

The inner side of the braid is next sewn, and here it must be gathered a little to fit the curve at the top; this is done by overcasting the edge of the braid through the tiny holes there, taking up the net after every third stitch. The stems are next worked in twist stitch with the embroidery cotton. Commence at the centre of the clover and run the needle in and out through every second mesh over the line for the stem, at the top turn back and run the thread under each stitch over the meshes down to the beginning.

Now make the padded rings for the centres by winding the embroidery thread around a small mesh 10 or 12 times, and work a row of buttonhole stitch closely around it, or the stitching may be done with a crochet-hook if preferred. One of these is sewn over the centre of each clover and at intervals on the net above the design.

Remove the lace from the design by cutting the threads on the back of the paper. Pick out all loose threads and cut away the net outside the margin of two or three meshes; top-sew the pearl edging on the wrong side, taking up the entire margin with the stitches. The neck part is inserted in a band of folded muslin, and neatly stitched in place.

The collar is now ready for filling in the lace stitches, which may be any with which you are familiar, or may be omitted if wished, but the more work put into the lace the more valuable it is. Many of the stitches shown on pages 6 and 7 would do for this, and can readily be copied.

# A Fine Crochet Medallion.

Use No. 80, Hicks, Bullick and Co.'s Irish Crochet Lace Thread.

Make 12 ch, form into a ring, into which put 16 loops of 18 ch each, turn, 9 ch 1 d c into top of loop, 4 ch 1 d c into each loop, turn, * 2 ch 1 d c into first loop, 4 ch 1 d c into each loop*, repeat until there is only one loop in the row. 2 ch 1 d c into the top loop, 6 ch 1 d c into same loop into one side of this loop put 8 loops of 16 ch each, turn.

8 ch 1 d c into top of first loop, 4 ch 1 d c into each loop, turn, * 2 ch 1 d c into top of first loop, 4 ch 1 d c into each loop, repeat from * until there is only one loop, then slip-stitch down the side to the top loop and work another leaf exactly like this into the other half of loop.

Break off the thread and fasten it to the first small loop on the large leaf at the right hand side, work d c closely into the loops along the side, putting a 5 ch picot into the centre of the d c on the first and every alternate loop.

Make 8 ch to reach first loop on the small leaf, then work the same edging around, reaching the ring at the other side with 8 ch; finish the remainder in the same way down to the point opposite the beginning. 9 ch 1 d c into the foundation ring, work d c closely into one half of the remaining portion of ring, then make a length of ch stitches about one and a half inches, 1 d c into the ring; now make a length of ch stitches to reach the top of this loop, fasten with a d c, turn and work d c closely over the three lengths of ch for the stem, finish the ring with d c and fasten off the thread securely on the back.

# Crochet Points.

These would do for dress collars, or blouse fronts, or night-dress collars, or for d'oileys.

**A Close Scallop.**

Use Ardern's No. 36 Cotton. Hook No. 5.

**Work the Top or Inside First.**

*1st Row.*—Make * 3 tr into 2nd loop on the edge of braid, 7 ch, 3 tr into fifth loop on braid, 3 ch, 3 long tr (thread twice over needle) into the bar on braid connecting the ovals, 3 ch to next oval. Repeat from *.

A CLOSE SCALLOP.

7 ch, 3 long tr into the d c below, 1 ordinary tr into the other 7 ch in row below.

**For the Lower or Outside Edge.**

*1st Row.*—Make * 1 d c into first loop on braid, 4 ch, 1 tr into next loop, 5 ch, 1 long tr into third loop, 6 ch, 1 long tr into fourth loop, 5 ch, 1 ordinary tr into fifth loop, 4 ch, 1 d c into sixth loop, 3 ch, 2 d c into bar connecting ovals, 3 ch. Repeat from *.

The only difference at corner is 4 d c into the bar each side of point, instead of the usual 2 d c.

*2nd Row.*—4 d c into the 4 ch below;

SPIDER WEB SCALLOP.

To turn the corner, make 2 tr into the second, third, fourth and fifth loop on oval; no ch between.

*2nd Row.*—* 5 tr into the top of the third tr in row below. 7 ch, 4 d c into ch below, 7 ch, 5 tr in top of the 3 tr below, 5 ch. Repeat from *. For corner: Make enough d c to carry right across without drawing in, with 7 ch each side connecting the d c with the 5 tr.

*3rd Row.*—Alternately make 7 ch and 14 ch, catching each time into the 7 ch below with 2 d c. For corner: 1 tr in last

AN OPEN SCALLOP.

3 d c, 4 ch (forming a picot), 3 d c
into the 5 ch. Into the 6 ch in
previous row make 4 tr, 4 ch, 2 long
tr, 4 ch, 2 long tr, 4 ch, 4 ordinary tr.

*3rd Row.*—* Into each of the 4 ch
(at the point and one each side) make
7 tr. Ch 7, catch in bar, ch 7 and
carry down to next scallop. Repeat
from *.

*4th Row.*—Over each 7 tr make 9
ch. Fill the ch to and from the
connecting bar with d c.

*5th Row.*—Put * 11 tr into the three
9 ch, fill the ch on each side with d c
till you reach the d c in previous row.
Then ch 10, catch back to fifth ch to
form a picot, ch 5, catch across into
next scallop. Fill the 9 ch in next
scallop with d c and repeat from *.

**An Open Scallop.**

Use Ardern's No. 36 Cotton and No.
5 Hook.

### For the Inside Edge.

*1st Row.*—* 2 tr in second loop of
braid, 2 ch, 1 tr in third loop, 2 ch, 1
tr in fourth loops 2 ch, 2 tr in fifth
loop. 7 ch, 3 long tr over bar, 7 ch.
Repeat from *. When turning the
corner, work an oval as follows : 2 tr
into second loop, 2 ch, 1 tr into third
loop, 2 ch, 1 tr into fourth loop, 2 ch,
now make 1 tr into third loop of next
oval, 2 ch, 1 tr into fourth loop, 2 ch,
2 tr into fifth loop, etc.

*2nd Row.*—2 d c into each 2 ch, 2
d c into one side of the 7 ch below,
then cross over the long tr below
with 7 ch, and put 2 d c into other
side.

### For the Outside Edge.

*1st Row.*—1 d c into each loop on
braid, with 5 ch between. Then 10
ch. catch back into fifth for a picot,
5 ch, and 1 d c into next oval. At the
corner make two picot ch with 3 long
tr over bar in between.

*2nd Row.*—* Into each of the 5 sp
of network put 2 d c with 5 ch
between. Then 7 ch to carry you to
the picot loop, into this make 3 loops
of 14 ch each, then 7 ch and repeat
from *.

*3rd Row.*—Into each sp of network
put 2 d c with 5 ch between. 7 ch to
each long loop with 2 d c into each
loop. Corner: 7 ch and 4 d c each
side of the 2 d c.

*4th Row.*—Put 7 tr into each 7 ch,
and 2 ch between each group of 7.
3 d c in middle sp of network. Corner:
7 ch to and from middle of the d c.

*5th Row.*—From the 3 d c in middle
to the 2 ch make 9 ch over each 7 tr.
Corner: Fill each 7 ch with d c.

*6th Row.*—Over the 2 top sets of 7
tr make 11 tr in the 9 ch. In the 9 ch
each side 9 d c. 3 ch across corner.

## Spider Web Scallop.

Suitable for nightdress collars,
cuffs, pillow-shams, etc.

Use Hicks, Bullick & Co.'s No. 40
Shamrock Crochet Cotton.

Select a braid with solid lobes
having 3 picots at one side of each
lobe and 2 at the other. Arrange the
braid with the angle and sew neatly
and securely in place. With the
crochet cotton, 1 d c into the centre
picot on a lobe, 18 ch 1 d c into same
picot, * 16 ch, miss next picot, 18 ch
loop into next 2 picots by taking the
two together, repeat from * putting a
loop into the corner picot and the 16
ch into the picot before and after.

*2nd Row.*—Into each 18 ch loop put
3 similar loops. 18 ch between the
loops.

*3rd Row.*—* 1 d c into the first of
3 loops, 10 ch picot 6 of them, 3 ch, 1
d c into next loop, 18 ch 1 d c into
same loop, 10 ch picot 6 of them, 3

ch, 1 d c into next loop, 1 d c over the centre of the loop between, 1 d c into first of next three. Repeat from *.

*4th Row.*—Fasten the thread to the centre of the first middle loop, * 18 ch, 1 d c into next middle loop, into which put 7 of these loops of 18 ch each, and repeat from *.

*5th Row.*—* 1 d c over first 18 ch bar, 1 d c into first loop, 7 ch 1 d c into second loop, 18 ch loop into this and four following loops with 5 ch between, 7 ch 1 d c into seventh loop, 1 d c over centre of next bar. Repeat from *, putting a picot bar between the groups of 10 ch picot 6, 3 ch.

*6th Row.*—* Into each of the 5 loops of last row put another of 18 ch with 7 ch between the loops, 9 ch into the picot, 9 ch and repeat from *.

*7th Row.*—Into the top of each of the 5 loops put 2 d c 5 ch 2 d c, 7 ch between the loops, 12 ch fastened to the d c over the picot, 12 ch and repeat from the first. This completes the lower edge.

*1st Top Row.*—Into the first of 2 picots over the first lobe put * 3 long tr, 5 ch, 3 long tr into next picot, 3 ch 1 d c into second next picot, 3 ch and repeat from *.

*2nd Row.*—3 tr over the 5 ch, 14 ch 3 tr into every 5 ch sp. Omit the chs between the trs at the corner.

# For Costume Trimming.

The wide fancy braids for trimming coats are very fashionable, and the better class of these trimmings are, of course, hand-made. The latest braid has an

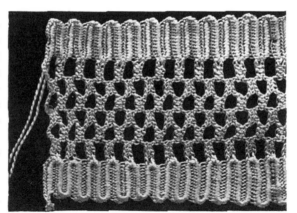

A Good Wearing Crochet Braid.

d c, over the padding, 1 ch, miss 1 ch, 3 d c into next 3 ch, 5 ch, miss 5, 3 d c into next 3 ch, 5 ch, miss 5, 3 d c into next· 3 ch, 5 ch, take up the cord and put 12 d c over

open fancy-work centre, and this can be very quickly worked by making two lengths of padding cord of coarse cotton thread, twisting the strands together.

Commence by inserting the hook in the end of one of the cords, and with crochet silk-thread of the required colour work 14 d c over the cord, 25 ch, take up the second piece of cord, and put 14 d c over it, turn, miss first 2, 1 d c into each of next

it into next 12 d c, * turn, 2 d c over the cord alone, 1 d c into each of the 12, 1 ch, miss 1 ch, 3 d c into next 3, 5 ch, miss 1 ch after the d c's, 3 d c into next 3, and repeat this into next sp, 5 ch, take up the padding at this side and work 12 d c over it into the d c's, and repeat from *.

This braid is also used for belts, and may be mounted on a suitable riband for that purpose if liked.

# A Baby's Kimono in Chain=Treble Stitch.

One ounce of white Shetland wool, half an ounce of pink wool of the same kind, and a No. 1 steel crochet hook are required.

The "chain-treble" stitch is made thus: having a loop already on the needle, insert the hook through two portions of the top of the tr or ch stitch below, draw the thread through, thread over the needle and through the last loop, thread over the needle again and through last ch loop, thread over the needle, and then draw it through the two loops still on the needle. In a long ch-tr form 3 ch loops before finally drawing the thread through last 2 loops.

Commence with 56 ch, always turn with 3 ch, insert the hook under two portions of 56th ch, and make 1 ch-tr, * 3 ch-tr into next ch, 1 ch-tr into next ch, miss next ch, 1 ch-tr into next, repeat from *, ending with 1 ch-tr.

2nd row, 3 ch, miss first ch-tr, 1 ch-tr into next, 5 ch-tr into next, * 1 ch-tr into next, miss next 2 ch-tr, ch-tr into next, 5 ch-tr into next, and repeat from *, ending the row with 1 ch-tr as at the beginning.

3rd and each succeeding alternate row, put 3 tr into the centre tr of the 5 tr, 1 tr into each of the others, missing the two at the narrowings, and ending each row with the same number of tr after the last, increasing tr as at the beginning of that row.

4th row and each succeeding alternate row, put 5 tr into the centre of the 3 tr in the preceding row, and 1 tr into each of the others, missing the two at the narrowings, and ending with the same number of tr after the last increasing as at the beginning.

After the 16th row, work as far as the narrowing stitches after the sixth vandyke, turn back to the corresponding stitch after the second vandyke, insert the hook in the first stitch of the third vandyke immediately after the preceding narrowing and work round to form the sleeve; there should be 18 rows in this sleeve portion from the first row.

Still working round, form the first row of the edging with the white thread, using the long ch-tr as already described, 1 long ch-tr into first tr, miss next tr, * 4 long tr into next tr, miss next tr, 1 long ch-tr into next,

miss next tr, and repeat from *.

Break off the thread and fasten it to the last stitch in the first row of the sleeve and continue working over the back part, and as far as the end of the third last vandyke, turn and work the second sleeve as the first. Join the thread to the last stitch of the 17th row at the end of the first row in this sleeve and complete this row, turn and continue working the front and back portions until 25 rows are formed from the beginning.

Work the white row for the edging as in the sleeves.

For the pink edging form a long ch-tr into each stitch of the foundation ch at the neck, continue down the front edge, putting 5 long ch-tr into each loop formed by the 3 ch at the turnings, at the lower end put 5 long ch-tr into the centre of the 4 ch-tr of the white row, work up the other front as in the first, and around the neck part put the 5 ch-tr into the spaces between every third and fourth tr.

Finish with a picot row, 1 d c into first tr, * 4 ch, picot three of these by putting a d c into the first ch, 1 d c into next tr, and repeat from *.

A narrow white silk riband is run in and out through the first row of long ch-tr for a drawstring at the neck.

# The Newest Thing in Crochet Belts.

These Crochet Silk Belts are being much worn. They are worked over

little bone rings, half-an-inch across, in d c with silk crochet thread any colour liked. Work only half way around each until sufficient are joined for the length of the belt, and put 3 d c over the stitch between the rings after the first stitch on the following ring, turn and complete the other half in the same way. In the second row join to the first in the centre of the half, and join the third in the same way. The buckle is only an ordinary metal one worked over closely with d c and a second row of 1 d c 5 tr 1 d c worked into the first.

**If this Fancy Stitchery Book has pleased you, and you are interested in high-class needlework, a number of original designs in Crochet, Knitting, Lace Stitches, Drawn-Thread Work, Tatting, and all forms of Embroidery, appear in the Girl's Own Paper and Woman's Magazine, which every month gives special attention to needlecraft.**

CURTIS AND BEAMISH, LTD., PRINTERS, COVENTRY.

# BARBOUR'S

## LINEN THREADS

—FOR—

## Lace, Knitting or Crochet Work.

**BEST**

*On Spools or
in* **1d.** *Skeins.*

**QUALITY**

*WHITE,
Nos. 30-100.*

## BARBOUR'S Popular "F.D.A."

### LINEN CROCHET THREAD.

*Crochets easily and produces exquisite work.*

In Nos.
8-100
White,
Cream,
Ecru,
Paris Grey.

—

**All Nos.
3d.**
per Ball.

Each Ball
is put up
in
dust-proof
holder
**without
extra charge**

To be had at all Needlework Depôts—or write to Mills direct (mentioning this book) for free samples and address of nearest Depôt.

**Wm. BARBOUR & SONS, Ltd., LISBURN, Ireland.**

# RELIABLE

# PAPER  PATTERNS

If you are wanting absolutely Reliable Paper Patterns of Coats, Evening Cloaks, Tailored Gowns, Dressy Frocks, Day or Evening Blouses, Underwear, Aprons, Dressing Gowns, or Children's Garments write to the

## FASHION  EDITOR
——— of the ———

# GIRL'S OWN PAPER and

# WOMAN'S  MAGAZINE

The Paper Pattern Department
——— of this Magazine ———

can supply the widest variety of Paper Patterns all of reliable cut and latest style.

## Price **4d.** each.
### Postage Extra.

**Address: THE FASHION EDITOR, 4, BOUVERIE ST., LONDON, E.C.**

# A MONTHLY BUDGET

—OF—

# STORIES

*HUMOROUS*
*PATHETIC*
*EXCITING*
*TENDER*

## FOR ALL READERS

4 ½ d.
NET
MONTHLY

## EVERYONE'S STORY MAGAZINE

**What they say about EVERYONE'S STORY MAGAZINE**

**Christian World** says : "It is solid value for 4½d."

**Methodist Recorder** says : "It is intensely readable."

**Newsagent** says : "The stories are really capital."

**Financial Times** says : "It should find a ready place among readers of light fiction."

**Standard** says : "It meets the demand for cheap, light, wholesome literature."

**Daily Graphic** says : "It is an uncommonly cheap fourpenny-ha'penny worth."

**Daily Telegraph** says : "It will please all leaders of condensed romance."

**Aberdeen Free Press** says : "The cover is attractive, the type handsome and legible."

**North Mail** says : "It is a charming companion, and a wonderful fourpence-halfpenny worth."

**Bookseller** says : "It is an excellent budget of fiction."

**Queen** says : "The stories are extremely readable."

**Daily News** says : "It may be specially recommended as a magazine for the family circle."

**North Devon Herald** says : "In every case the dramatis personæ are healthy and wholesome human beings, without a trace of the morbid quality from crown to finger-tip."

**Scotsman** says : "The tales reach a high standard."

# Hicks' Lace Threads

### MADE IN IRELAND, THE HOME OF LACE,

## for making IRISH CROCHET,
## CARRICKMACROSS & LIMERICK
## LACES.

**Used in the best LACE DISTRICTS in Ireland.**

*Stocked by the*
**NEW IRISH DIRECT SUPPLY, Ltd.,**
94, Victoria Street, London, S.W.

"SHAMROCK" CROCHET BALLS
and
"SHAMROCK" MACHINE REELS.

*Makers—*
**HICKS, BULLICK & CO., Ltd.,**
Sackville Thread Works, Belfast.
*(who invite enquiries
mentioning this book.)*

---

**FOURTH
EDITION
NOW
READY.**

Large Crown
8vo,

## 1/- net

(By post, 1/4).

# THE
# HOME
# ART
# CROCHET
# BOOK

**By FLORA
KLICKMANN**

Editor
of the

**GIRL'S OWN**
and

**WOMAN'S
MAGAZINE.**

Published
at
4, Bouverie
Street,
London, E.C.

THIS BOOK CONTAINS

**Entirely New Designs for Lingerie, Edgings
and Insertions.**
**Borders for Tray Cloths and D'oileys.**
**Deep Laces for Table Cloths and Valances**
**Motifs for Inlet Work and Irish Lace.**

Sold by
Booksellers
and
Fancy Work
Dealers
Everywhere.

N<sup>O</sup> Woman can afford to miss reading this Magazine. It is full of Stories and Papers in the highest degree interesting and helpful to Girls and Women of the Middle and Upper Classes.

**6**<sup>**D**</sup>**..**

**Monthly.**

The
Girl's Own
AND
Woman's
Magazine

Edited by
**FLORA
KLICKMANN**

" No praise can be too high for this Magazine. Each article is written with knowledge and insight, and in a practical spirit."—*Morning Post.*

" It is an absolute mine of information, as well as an excellent story journal."—*Lady's Pictorial.*

" The practical articles are especially good."—*Guardian.*

" Plenty of pleasant, wholesome fiction and practical information is to be found in this magazine."—*Spectator.*

*Papers on subjects of national and topical interest for women who think; Fancy Work Designs; Fashions: Reasonable and Seasonable.* - - - - - -

**On Sale
EVERY-
WHERE.**